Living Life After Death

Discover the Power to Survive after Death Occurs in Your Life

Cornelius D. Jones

Praise for Cornelius D. Jones's
Living Life after Death

"The chapter on Letting Go really spoke to me and what I went through last year with the loss of my dad. The chapter is easy to read, awe-inspiring, heartfelt, informative, touching, captivating and poignant.

-Keyyaunna Joiner New Orleans, LA

"This is a topic that many will appreciate Dr. Jones discussing. Peeling back the layers of grief is a process." *-Author Joy W. Simone*

"This book can help a person that has been through this type of situation."

-Tia Williams

"Very intriguing, a good book that I look forward to reading."

-Frank Joyner Jr. Memphis, TN

"I applaud and salute you for deciding to not just think outside the box, but kick it right on its side! This book is profound, relatable, spiritual, insightful and honest." *-Hawanya Render Educator in West Palm Beach*

"Awesome synopsis of the death and grievance process. Great read for those struggling to cope with the difficult stages of death."

-Brittany Dixon Licensed Funeral Director

Jones Productions Enterprises
Jacksonville, FL 32221

Cover design: C.D. Jones Books/Unique graphics design team

2014 edition: Janice Bradley editor

Publication date 8/14/2014

ISBN: 978-1-312-43575-9

Manufactured in the United States of America

Library of Congress Cataloging - in - Publication Data

Jones, Cornelius D

Living Life after Death: Discover the Power to Survive after Death Occurs in Your Life / Cornelius Jones. p.cm. www.corneliusdjones.org

Our mission is to create and distribute inspirational products offering exceptional value and encouragement to the masses.

Table of Contents

Acknowledgments 6

Introduction 7

CHAPTER 1- The Survivor 10

CHAPTER 2- Death Changes Life 17

CHAPTER 3- Understanding Death 29

CHAPTER 4- Facing Grief 34

CHAPTER 5- Acknowledge You're Grieving 42

CHAPTER 6- The Power to Survive 72

CHAPTER 7- Finding Peace 77

CHAPTER 8- Letting Go 90

Appendix 105

ACKNOWLEDGMENTS

TO THE FIRST EDITION

THE PEOPLE LISTED BELOW all commented on CHAPTERs, suggested sources, corrected my mistakes, or provided other moral or material aid. There were so many who offered encouragement, provided feedback and supported my vision on this project. I thank you very much. They are: Frank Joyner Jr., Tia Williams, Keyyaunna Joiner, Joy Simone, Brittany Dixon, and last but not least Hawanya Render, It is such a blessing to have people that I know that I can count on to give me the truth when I need to hear it the most.

There are so many others that are worthy of being acknowledged in this section. I'm thankful for the countless men and women that work as chaplains, pastors, ministers, counselors, social workers, life coaches, and mental health professionals to help individuals and their families to cope with the difficulties of life. Your commitment and dedication to meet the needs of others may not always get the attention that it deserves but please understand that you are all appreciated for what you do.

Introduction

 Life and death are interconnected in a very mysterious way that we must try our best to accept and understand. Life brings joy and promise as we witness the innocence of a baby as they are born into this world. Death on the other hand causes us to pause in thought as we mourn over the loss of those who mean so much to us. Unless we are the individual that is getting buried our life does not stop just because our loved ones are now in death.

As I sat to write this book, I wrote it knowing that I'm leaving my own love ones with a guide filled with information that they will one day have to turn to after my loss to pick up the pieces and move forward. I'm a father, husband, son, brother, and friend that will leave those who love me in mourning in the future. Although I can't do anything to stop my own death from occurring, I have come to understand that I can make it easier for them to live life after I'm gone by leaving words of encouragement.

This book has taken me six years to muster the strength to complete. After dealing with the loss of my brother alone and keeping my feelings and thoughts about his death locked away in the private vault that rest in the corner of my mind, I came to understand that there are others who are wrestling with similar challenges to that of my own. I knew that I needed to write not for myself but for the millions of people that still search for the strength to get up and face another day.

"Living Life after Death," is a book created to offer support and help those who are living with the pain that death has caused in their lives. I wanted to provide you with ways to progress through this journey of difficulty and remind you that although the life of your love one has ended you must learn to keep living after death has occurred.

"They that love beyond the world cannot be separated by it. Death cannot kill what never dies." ~ **Williams Penn**

CHAPTER 1

The Survivor

I am a survivor of one the most challenging ordeals that anyone could go through which is death. Let me be clear from the beginning, I have not survived death because I wanted to but because I had to in order to function in a normal manner. I've experienced, accepted, and beat death several times during the course of my life. After losing a parent, sibling, family members, close friends, and co-workers to death I understand the level of strength, and faith that it takes to be able to push forward after such losses.

Unlike other survivors there are no ribbons to pin on my chest, special colored decals reserved to place on the back of my vehicles, or support groups to symbolize what I have been through with death so that the world can see that I'm too a survivor. Although I'm well aware of the treatment plans, support systems, strength, will power and resilience that people who battle with Cancer, Aids, ALS, Alzheimer, sexual assault, drug a and alcohol additions, along with the other chronic illnesses must have in order to fight for a chance at survival. I just don't think that many of us fully understand or fail to respect what it takes for anyone to survive the reality of death.

I do not want to mislead anyone and leave them with the false impression that I myself, died and somehow came back to life. I am not immune to death and possess no form of supernatural powers which will ever prevent me from dying. I know and accept that when God is ready for me to leave this earth that it will happen and there will be nothing that I can do to prevent it.

I will share with you that in 2007 I had a very close death experience that shook up my whole world. On February 7, 2007 I underwent open heart surgery to correct a heart condition known as Atrial-Fibrillation. Normally this condition can be managed with medication, but due to my heart not responding well to the medicine we all felt it was in my best interest to have open heart surgery performed. The surgical maze procedure had a very high success rate and would give me a better chance of living a normal life.

The surgery went as planned and I remained hospitalized for a few days before being discharged to go home. At the time of my release, I was left with the sad truth that in only a few short days I would be on my own and without anyone there to assist me. I can honestly say that it felt like me against the world. Originally there was a plan in place to have someone by my side during the entire recovery process, needless to say that plan fell apart at the seams only days prior to the operation. I was fortunate enough to have someone with me for the first few days after the surgery and for that I'm forever grateful because those were indeed some of the most challenging days of my life.

After leaving the hospital, I was driven back to the hotel that I was staying in when I first arrived back to the United States from Japan only a few weeks earlier. I can recall going to lie down after making it back into the room because my body could not produce enough energy for me to do anything else. At that moment it dawned on me for the first time as an adult that I might be in trouble trying to take care of myself. I have always been a firm believer that tough times don't last always but tough people do. In my mind I knew that since there would not be anyone with me that I needed to be as tough as I could to make it through that period. I later discovered that it would be that very belief that would take me to the edge of life.

Everything that I once did with ease and never gave a second thought to doing had suddenly become very difficult to do on my own. Sitting up was hard standing up was a task, and walking more than a couple of feet seemed to be manual labor. I was still in my twenties but my body felt as if it had aged 40 years over my hospital stay. I did my best to follow the discharge paperwork, which instructed me to take short walks a few times a day to try to build endurance and get my heart use to some level of activity again.

On the second day of being in the hotel room, I developed a really bad cough that sucked the life out of me every time that I did it. I also noticed that I would pass out after coughing because the coughs were so intense. No matter how many times this strange activity happened I dismissed it and just figured that it was a normal part of the recovery process. I later realized that it was due to my lungs not being completely open and filled with fluids as the result of the operation which caused me to develop pneumonia. That evening the coughing and fainting spells continued and I knew that I had to some way get back to the hospital or I would likely die. Just as I began to try to force myself out of the bed, it happened again and I was out and fell on the floor.

I remember coming back to consciousness while I was in the emergency room with doctors standing around me discussing what they thought caused me to return so soon. One of the doctors noticed that my eyes were open and asked me if I could try to explain to them what was going on with me. I knew that I was not in any condition to explain anything, but I still tried to do my very best to be helpful. As I begin to tell them of what I was experiencing, my body decided to show them instead so they could witness it for themselves. After waking up again I discovered that I was in the process of having a CT scan done on my brain because the doctors thought that there was neurological reason in my head that was causing me to suddenly pass out.

After the tests were complete, they apparently didn't see anything abnormal that offered any explanation to what was going on. I was taken to a room where a neurologist, cardiologist, and a few other doctors came in to talk to me. I recall asking the doctors, "why are you all upside down?" One of the doctors asked me, "what do you mean that we are upside down?" I tried to explain but suddenly felt like I needed to go to the rest room right away. I asked for assistance to get up, but as I stood up I felt extremely lightheaded before blood started pouring down my hospital gown unto the floor. This was the last thing that I remember before I collapsed again.

When I passed out that time it was much different than the times before, I felt a peace that is unexplainable. I did not feel myself floating, but I knew of no pain. The discomfort that I had just experience only moments before was gone and for the first time in days I liked the way that I felt because I felt whole again. There was nothing threating or scary about the situation that I was in. It was a complete state of calmness that I can only describe as beautiful serenity.

I witnessed portions of my life both positive and negative moments going back to my childhood that I had simply forgotten about. They ran through my mind as if I was watching a movie of some kind. When I explained it someone years later they told me that it sounded like I had a near death experience and possibly even died, but was spared to be given a second chance at life. Looking back on it, I never felt like I had actually died, but I am sure that I during that time I became closer to the Lord as the result of the experience.

I woke up in the Intensive Care Unit with tubes down my throat, I reached to pull the tube out because I felt as I was gagging and could not get enough air. I also wanted to call my mother and tell her that I planned to answer the call to minister. Unknown to myself at the time, I had just awaken from what was called a short coma and I was being monitored around the clock for any signs of progress. The nurse in the room quickly grabbed my hands and urged me not to pull at the tubes as she pressed the emergency button for help so that I could be sedated to calm me down.

It was later explained to me what happened lead me back to the hospital so quickly. Fluid build-up from the first operation surrounded my heart and would not allow it to pump properly. One of my lungs had nearly collapsed which explained why when I coughed I passed out. Everything seemed to be explainable except for what I experienced when I was absent from my body. I simply came to except that men who rely on medical explanations to understand everything could not possibly understand supernatural experiences and I elected to accept my unique experience as a gift from God.

Some may conclude that maybe what I experienced really was a form of death. I have never gone into any detail of what I truly experienced until now. I will never understand why God allowed me to have had the experience that I did but I know that it was for a purpose. There are many testimonies of people who has been pronounced clinically dead and who can join me in sharing their near – death experience. For example in **90 Minutes in Heaven** Don Piper, gave his personal testimony of his near - death experience. He reported that the EMT's on the scene determined that he was he been killed instantly after a tractor-trailer had swerved into his lane, crushing his car. (Murphy, Piper 2004) Piper survived, however, and later claimed that he saw loved ones and friends as well as magnificent light; he felt a sense of pure peace.

My personal experience with actual death initially didn't afford me with the opportunity to feel the sense of peace that I felt when I was hospitalized back in 2007 or that which Mr. Piper made mention of. Like so many others who have been forced to face death alone I was reminded that death comes with a great deal of pain. It made me come to the realization that when we are born into this world we are born alone in a sense, so we each must figure out how to deal with death alone, but only in a way that allows us to mourn properly.

I have often said that when a child is expected to be born, the hospital room is filled with family members, and a medical staff that is anticipating the birth of the new addition to the family, and everyone is anxious for the baby's arrival. The tragedy is that too many times when someone passes away there is no one there to comfort them as they depart this earth and even worse there is no one there to truly comfort the family that the deceased have left behind.

It has been estimated that 55.3 million people die a year according to the U.S Census Bureau, International Programs Center. These are the most recent statics as of 2012 which means that somewhere there are millions of mothers, fathers, brothers, sisters, children, grandchildren, uncles, aunties, cousins, friends, or co-workers who are left to mourn their losses alone. I do not want anyone else to feel that they are alone in life just because they have lost someone to death. I have felt that feeling and I know that it is not a pleasant feeling to have.

I'm pleased to tell you today that I am a survivor who felt a pain that I did not know that a human being could even feel. I'm familiar with the hurt, struggled with the need to have answers and know the feeling of being a victim. I am not ashamed to tell you that there were periods of darkness, loneliness, and a bitterness that was so overwhelming that I could not wrap my mind around anything positive or good. I survived because I found things that I could do that would occupy my mind to help me to heal. I will tell you that in order to accomplish becoming a survivor you must commit yourself to surviving at all cost.

CHAPTER 2

Death Changes Life

Life couldn't have being going any easier for me in March of 2008. I had just been transferred to the North Chicago's Great Lakes community on a 3 year work assignment. I was still physically trying to adjust to the drastic climate change that the state of Illinois so harshly forces newcomers to accept. After living in the comfort of beautiful San Diego, CA. for over a year I had almost forgotten what winter weather felt like. Thanks to good old Mother Nature, I was quickly reminded of the torture that winter weather creates.

Throughout the day the sky was always gloomy as if the clouds seemed to have conspired against the Sun to keep it from coming out to offer any relief of warmth. I can recall how the temperature would drop so low in the evenings that it made it so challenging for me to do anything but rush to my car and head directly home to shield my body away from the cold. The roads were always covered with feet of snow, which camouflaged the deteriorated roads that seemed to be spotted with potholes and huge cracks from the salt and snowplows that worked around the clock to make it safe to drive. I will admit that the city did the best job that it could to keep the streets clear and safe, but the city's defense system to fight the constant ambush of snow also created damage that caused much frustration for the citizens and drivers of the state of Illinois.

Although I resented the winter weather, I was very eager to get settled in to the new community. I felt that once I did, that maybe I would feel better about my choice to move there. Every day I questioned myself on why had I left the beautiful weather of southern California to go to a place as dreadful North Chicago? No matter how many times I asked myself the question the answer always seemed to be the same which ended in me shaking my head while saying "what was I thinking to do this to myself?"

The thing that I knew was since I was already there I had better make the best of the situation. I went through a laundry list of things that I wanted to do that were in alignment with my personal goals. I had just completed my master's degree only months earlier and I knew that school was not something that I wanted to jump right back into. Financially I was pretty stabled and did not see any need to do anything different than what I was already doing. I decided to take a stab at homeownership and applied for a loan to purchase. I knew that I had no intentions of settling down in the area and would only use any house that I bought there as an income property. The loan was approved and the search was now officially on.

I contacted a realtor and began looking for a home in the Hyde Park area. I knew that my assignment was only for three years and to most people including my realtor the decision to buy a home there did not make much sense knowing that I would only be there for such a short period of time. Honestly I could not stomach the thought of tossing my money in the trash by paying rent for a piece of property that I could never own.

After looking at house after house, day after day I finally saw one that I just had to have. There were a couple of pros and cons to the property but they were not deal breakers for me. At the time there were multiple offers on the house so I knew that I had to give it my best shot if I expected to come out as the winner. I studied comparative homes in the area to make sure that my bid would not be an insult to the sellers but also making sure that I was not making a foolish offer by over paying. I decided to go $2,500 over what the counter offer was but I also knew that my guaranteed VA loan gave me an advantage because it was no way that the loan could flop on my end as long as the home passed the inspection. After careful consideration, I held out a few more days to see what would happen with the other buyers before letting the sellers know that I was willing to bid higher if necessary.

On March 28, 2008 I decided to make my final offer on the home. As always, I said a prayer and I told God that if it was meant to be that I knew that He would make sure everything went smoothly. I've always been a man of faith and trusted that whatever I prayed about would be heard and answered by God. That evening we found out that two of the other buyers had withdrew their offers and at the time there were no other offers on the table better than my original one. My agent and I felt really good about my chances to get the property so we put the wheels into motion. My agent assured me that he would notify me as soon as he found out anything from the seller and from that moment forward the wait was on.

It was around noon on Sunday March 30th when I received a phone call from my agent asking me would I be able to meet with him because he had some news that he wanted to share with me about the home. We ended up meeting at a Starbucks; my agent came in and asked me if I was sure that the property in Hyde Park was the only home that I wanted? He went on to tell me that I had to be certain about the house because he did not want me to have any regrets later. I confirmed that it was the home that I wanted, and I asked him "is there something wrong or that I need to know about the property?" My agent said no there was nothing wrong and yes that there was something that I needed to know. He told me that my offer had been accepted and then congratulated me on my purchase of the home.

As you can imagine I was elated and filled with joy that things had gone the way that I expected them to. I could not wait to share the wonderful news with my family but I figured that I could just call and tell them later that evening when everyone would be home and settled in.

I decided to go out to celebrate this wonderful news but I knew that since it was on a Sunday and everyone had to work the next day, all we could do was go and grab a good meal. I contacted a couple of my new co-workers and we all planned to meet up at the local Cracker Barrel to hang out and eat. Once we made it to the restaurant I told everyone the good news and we began making plans for the housewarming party. As we sat talking and laughing I suddenly became very uneasy, but it wasn't from anything that any of the guys had said but yet the feelings was still unexplainable. I wasn't sure what it was or why I felt the way that I did, but I also knew that there was something unusual going on that related to me that created the feeling.

After we had eaten the rest of the group remained laughing and talking in the restaurant, but I decided that it was time for me to leave since my mood had suddenly changed. The guys tried to convince me to stay and asked why was I leaving so soon? I don't quite remember exactly what I told them but I am sure it was some generic form of the truth to get me out of there as quick as possible.

Once I made it back to my car I noticed that my cell phone which had been left inside the car had an abundance of missed calls. At the first glance I did not realize that all of the calls were either from my family or people that I had grown up with. Since I was driving and the road conditions were very poor I figured that it would be best until I made it back to the base before I tried to return any of the missed calls or even listen to the voicemails that had been left for me.

After parking my car I decided to go through the voicemails, the first couple of messages did not reveal anything as the messengers simply encouraged me please call back when I felt like talking. The next message was from my sister, I could tell by the tone in her voice that something was going on but I guess due to circumstances her words sounded muffled in the recording as she pleaded with me in her message to call home because it was an emergency. I immediately called and asked her "what's wrong?" and she replied "he is gone our baby brother is dead!" I yelled out to her hoping that what she had just said was a mistake. I immediately called my mother, she confirmed that he was dead and before I knew it I flew into a rage yelling words that I had not used in a number of years. I demanded to know what happened to him, but the details of his death was uncertain which only added to my anger and hurt. The pain was so overwhelming that I sat in my car for an hour or so just crying and beating on the steering wheel and dashboard asking God why, why, why?

At some point the police surrounded my car because they were called and told that someone was in the car screaming. One of the officers tapped on the driver's side window and asked me to step out of the car. I couldn't move and the time was not right for anyone to bother me. I rolled down my window frowned up with tears streaming down my face and I told them that I was not trying to be disrespectful but my little brother had just been killed and I needed to be alone. With my window barely cracked, the officers offered their condolences and of the asked if I had anyone that I could call because I was in no condition to be alone. I remember telling him that I had a supervisor that I could call but I was still not getting out of my vehicle.

The officers were very understanding and told me that it was fine for me to stay in my car until someone arrived to sit with me. Two of the officers sat in their patrol unit keeping a close eye on me until my supervisor came. They spoke to him briefly before they all came back to my car. The officers told me that they were sorry for my loss, shook my hand and told me that if I needed anything to call them. They handed me their cards before they walked back to their unit to leave.

After the officers left, my supervisor informed me that he had already notified the next person in our chain of command and told me that my emergency leave request would be ready for me to pick up the next morning. That was very kind of them to do what they could so I would be better prepared to go and be with my family without any protocol delays. He also invited me to come to stay the night at his home with his family. I remember walking in and the look on his wife's face told me that she already knew of the hurt that I was going through. She offered me food, told me that her and her family was there for me if I needed or wanted to talk. She encouraged me to use their phone to call my family and to talk as long as I needed. The couple told me that the guest room was available for me lay down whenever I was ready, they prayed with me before retiring for the evening.

That night I was not able to get much sleep as my mind raced back and forwards thinking about my only little brother being dead. I looked back on our relationship and the unique bond that he and I have always had. I thought about the time that we had just spent together back in Atlanta and the wonderful week we shared. I also thought about the heartache that my mother must have been going through and how she needed her children by her side more than ever before.

Early the next morning, I went to pick up my leave paperwork, withdrew funds and headed down south to be with my family. The weather conditions were far from favorable as the snow fell from the sky in every direction imaginable. There was a bad winter storm going on, and it was predicted to get worse as the day continued. With little concern for my own safety I found myself driving in the middle of one of the worse winter storms of the year. I was blinded by the need to be with my family, and did not care about anything other than getting to them so a little snowstorm was not going to stop me.

As I was driving, when I was not breaking down crying, my mind was too busy drifting back to my brother for me to focus on the road. I know in my heart that I must of had angels driving and looking out for me on such a dangerous road. I had barely gotten a couple of hours of sleep the night before, so I kept dozing off as I struggled to fight the need to sleep. I drank a few 5 hour energy drinks just to give myself some form of fuel. If you take into account the fact that I was drowsy, crying and daydreaming then it becomes apparent that I was not in control of my travels and it was only by the grace of God that I had not been in a horrible accident that could have resulted in my mother burying two of her children.

I talked to God on my drive and prayed for the strength of a thousand men because I knew that I would need to be strong for my mother, sister, and brothers during this most difficult time. I prepared in my mind my strategy to help me to accomplish that task without allowing them to see my own hurt or need to be comforted. Over the course of life I had come accustomed to withholding my emotions from others including my own family.

By the time that I made it to my destination safely, I had cried enough in private that I would be able to deal with his death in public without shedding a tear. My mother was still in Atlanta taking care of my brother's last affairs when I first made it to Grenada, Ms. I knew that I had an extra day to deal with my own emotions before I would have to push them back in the corner on the top shelf. It helped me that she was not there and I took full advantage of spending that time alone.

Once she arrived back to Mississippi, I was not at the house when she made it back to town, but there were others there to comfort her. As I pulled up at the house I witnessed the most broken hearted woman that I had ever seen standing in the yard. I observed people in the driveway trying to offer their condolences to her before I got out my car to walk to hug her. There were so many things that ran through my mind but none of them would be appropriate to say that could take away the pain that either one of us were feeling. I hugged her as tight as I had ever done before as we both just rocked from side the side. We knew in our hearts that this was just one of the many sad days ahead.

After making inside the house, my mother was restless, and my heart ached for her because I knew that the pain that she was trapped in would take years to go away. Later that day we went over Robinson & Son's Funeral home to see my brother's body that had been shipped from Atlanta to Grenada. I will never forget as the funeral director urged us that my brother was not in any condition to be seen, and told us that they had not done anything to his body since receiving him. The owner told us that they do not normally allow families to see the body until it has been prepared and dressed. He eventually gave in to my mother's pleas and said since she was his mother that he would allow us to see the body of my brother and her son.

Moments later the staff rolled my brother who was still nude with only a thin white sheet to partially cover him. I will never forget the image of him on the metal gurney in a cardboard box. I was in total disbelief that my brother was really gone until that moment seeing him there lifeless. The image of him from that moment has become a permanent photo in my mind that can't be erased. My mother cried out, "look at my baby" as she broke down again in tears. My older brothers who had driven down with her from Atlanta and I did what we could to comfort her. We each knew in our minds that it was nothing that we could do that would give her the comfort that she needed at the moment. After she had some time to look at him the director signaled for his staff to take my brother's body away.

Shortly after they came to remove him, we were escorted to look at coffins available for selection to bury him in. This has to be one of the most uncomfortable things that a family must deal with after the loss of a love one. Maybe it is the fact that we were left to choose a container to place our love one in only moments after seeing him in that condition. My mother wanted me to help her to select a coffin, I can only guess how hard the process was for her because it tore me up inside. I never knew that coffins are so expensive or come in so many different models.

After my mother had chosen the one that she was best satisfied with we went into discuss the financial arrangements, the cemetery price which was separate from the funeral home price, church location and other details. This process is far from pleasant but necessary prior to the funeral to make sure that everything is taken care of.

After leaving the funeral home I decided that I would go and look for something to bury my little brother in, I knew that he and I shared a similar fashion taste and I wanted to make sure that he looked good for the last time that anyone would see him on earth. I chose him a soft blue dress shirt to match the lining in his coffin, with a striped tie that shared the same color as the shirt accompanied with a matching handkerchief. I bought myself the exact same shirt, tie, and handkerchief because the same thing that I was prepared to bury him in was also good enough for me to wear in life.

The night before the funeral, after spending time with family members and close friends I decided to go back to the hotel that I was staying at to clear my head. I knew that I needed to spend time with the Lord in prayer because the next day would likely be the hardest day of my life.

Needed changes

After the funeral things seemed to change rather quickly. Once all the family members and friends said their goodbyes to my mother the reality sat in. She was left with nothing but her thoughts and was just as broken as she was the day that she found out that her youngest child had died. She demonstrated all of the symptoms of someone who was dealing with depression. She still wasn't sleeping or eating and it was apparent to me that once her surviving children returned back to our own homes that she would likely break completely down.

I was scheduled to report back to work in a couple of days but wrestled with leaving my mother knowing that she was in such pain. The day of my schedule departure I did all that I could to try to cheer her up prior to me leaving to go back to Illinois. I talked to her and told her that I promised to come back as often as possible and encouraged her to call me if she wanted to talk. She told me that it would take some time but she would be fine. We hugged and said our goodbyes prior to heading back on my long road trip.

As I was about 4 hours into my drive, the urge to return to Mississippi to be by my mother's side became stronger and stronger. I was uneasy knowing that she was left to deal with things on her own. It didn't seem right that she had 4 surviving kids and none of us was there with her during a time like that. I made a phone call to my supervisor to extend my leave and turned my car around in Arkansas to go and stand by my mother.

After being there for an additional couple of weeks, I felt good knowing that I was able to be there for her as she went through the emotional roller coaster. I did everything that I could to make her life easier as I continued to bottle up my own emotions. It was more important to me that she was ok than myself. I could tell that she appreciated my presence, and I knew that I was helping her by just being there. If I could have stayed longer I would have, but I knew that my leave days would eventually run out.

I was only a couple of weeks from closing on my new home but none of that no longer mattered to me. My only focus was getting closer to my mother and I knew that God would make a way for it to happen.

A week after returning to work, I was called into the administration office because it was determined by the medical staff that I needed to be reassigned to a place that could better serve my medical needs. I didn't put up any argument and knew that this had to be divine intervention. What was the chance of this happening the way that it was without it being the will of God?

I was reassigned to Louisiana which was only 5 hours away from where my mother lived which pleased the two of us. Although I never got the chance to get the keys to the home that I wanted, and would have to start all over again at least I was now closer my family so that I could offer more support.

My life changed in many ways in such a short period of time. I found myself doing things that I probably would have never considered prior to the death of my brother Gerry but I understood the significance of the changes that were needed.

Maybe the changes in your life weren't the same as mine, but I'm certain that if death occurred in your life that changes of some kind followed. Just as the birth of a child in a family changes things so does the death of a family member, friend, or coworker.

Make a list of 3-5 changes that you've noticed since the last or most significant loss has occurred in your life and develop an individual plan on how to turn those into healthy changes.
1.
2.
3.
4.
5.

CHAPTER 3

Understanding Death

Perhaps if we learn to understand death we could learn to accept it easier as a part of the process of life. In this short chapter I will provide you with the source that I turned to for my own healing. It is true that I've helped others with grief as a counselor for a number of years. I have studied an abundance of books written by man and women that are considered to be the subject matter experts in death. Although I do find their records of thoughts on death useful, I want you to know that I still rely on the Bible more than my own training or the teachings of others to understand death and why it is a necessary process.

Since life first began in the Bible, and death was promised there, I decided to turn to the oldest and most reliable source that I knew of to try to understand death better for myself so that my words on the subject would be able to benefit others. Throughout the bible you will find the word death hundreds of times which means it is something that we can all expect to occur at some point.

The biblical portrait of death is not that of normal outworking of natural processes. Instead, the Bible presents human death as a reaffirmation that something has gone awry in God's created order. The Scriptures do not, however picture death as a hopeless termination of human consciousness but instead brim with the hope of resurrection. Many biblical scholars group the Bible's teachings on death into three distinct but interrelated categories – physical, spiritual, and eternal. In this chapter I want to address the physical, spiritual, and eternal death.

Let's first take a look at physical death the opening chapters of the Pentateuch pinpoint the origin of human death in the Edenic rebellion (*Gen. 3:19*). The morality eventually overtook Adam and is a certainty for all his descendants. Apart from direct miraculous provision, as in the case of the prophet Elijah (*2 Kings 2:11*), God has fixed an hour of death for each human being (*Heb. 9:27*). In their fallen and finite state, human beings are powerless to avert the reality of death (*Ps. 89:48*).

The reality of death pervades the Scriptures. Within the Old Testament community, the touching of a corpse rendered an individual unclean (*Num. 5:2*). Even contact with the bones of the dead or with a grave necessitated seven days of ritual uncleanliness (*Num. 19:16*). The people of God were forbidden to mourn their departed with customs of their pagan nations around them such as ceremonial cutting of skin and head shaving (*Deut. 14:1*).

Since God is the giver of life, He has the sovereign prerogative to take human life at His own good pleasure. At times in the old covenant theocracy, God by direct revelation through His prophets appointed His people to exercise His judgment on the enemies of the people of God (*Num. 31: 1-11; Deut. 7:22-26; 20; 1 Sam. 15:1-8*). The new covenant church, however, was not given such authority. The church's power does not extend to bodily life or death but only to the power to expel unrepentant sinners from the body (*1 Cor. 5:9-13*). Even so, the Bible does not speak of death as a drastic manifestation of God's divine discipline over those within the believing community who remain unrepentant in their sinful activity. Death does not happen because of our sins, death happens because everything that is born or grows will someday die. That's the natural order of life.

Throughout the Bible, death is a reminder of the brevity of human life. The Bible calls for joyful living in light of one's certain destiny in the grave (*Eccles. 9:9-10*), compares the shortness of life to the fleeting existence of a flower (*Job 14:2*), and the contrast the shortness of human life with the eternal faithfulness of God (*Pss. 90:2-12; 103: 14-17*). Jesus spoke of the suddenness of death as a warning of to those who trust in their earthly possessions rather than in the gracious provision of God (*Luke 12:16-20*). James, describing human existence as a "vapor," argues that impending death exposes the tentativeness of all human plans.

The Bible nowhere presents physical death as a painless transition from material existence to the spiritual plane. Facing death of his friend Lazarus, for instance, Jesus did not react with a detached resignation but was moved to tears of compassion by the pain death had left in its wake (*John 11:35,38*). The Apostle Paul seems ambivalent about his own foreseen death at the hands of the state. The goodness he finds in death is not an escape from life. Rather, Paul rejoices in the knowledge that in death he both would glorify and be in the presence of His Messiah, the Lord Jesus Christ.

Scripture closely associates death with the malevolent activity of Satan, whom Jesus labeled a "murderer from the beginning" (*John 8:44 HCSB*). The entrance of death into the creation came through the cunning temptation of the serpent, go back and look at the book of Genesis to witness this evolution. The writer of Hebrews ascribes to the evil one the "power of death," namely a paralyzing and universal fear of death, from which believers are liberated by the atonement of Christ.

Although physical death is sometimes compared to sleep, Scripture does not teach that one's consciousness lapse after death to reawaken at the day of resurrection and judgment. Jesus promised the repentant thief on the cross that He would see paradise the very day of death (*Luke 23:43*). Paul teaches that, for believers being absent from the body means being present with Christ (*2 Cor. 5:8*).

Spiritual Death is the cataclysmic result of Adam's fall and is not limited to bodily death. The scripture characterizes fallen humanity as "dead in trespasses and sins." Human beings are born with the sentence of death hanging over our heads, but we are also born with corrupt desires and inclinations that render us completely "dead" to the peril of our own accumulating guilt.

As such, humans are alienated from our creator. The mind suppresses what can be clearly seen of God in His creation, preferring to worship idols. The will refuses to acknowledge the truth of God's self- disclosure (*Rom. 3:10*). The affections cling to sinful cravings, preferring them to the righteousness of God (*John 3:19; Phil. 3:19*). This spiritual deadness, if counteracted by the gracious activity of God in the gospel, will lead to eternal judgment.

In Eternal Death, the bodily death does not end the accountability of rebellious humans before the holy tribunal of God. After the appointed hour of death comes judgment (*Heb. 9:27*). The Bible goes on to use the word "death" at times to describe the wrath of God visited upon unbelievers in the afterlife. (*Rev. 20:14*). Though this hellish reality is sometimes called "perishing" (*John 3:16; 2 Pet. 2:12)* and destruction. It cannot be understood as the annihilation of the other person. In contrast with the momentary sting of physical death, the death that awaits the sinner at the last day of judgment.

After reading this chapter it is my prayer that you are have learned that although the Bible mentions death in a few different forms that when death does come it will be permanent for the body but not the soul. Since we know that the soul or spirit lives on we should rejoice knowing that just because the body which is shell is no longer in use that spirit still has life.

CHAPTER 4

Facing Grief

Losing someone or something you love is very painful. After a significant loss, you may experience all kinds of difficult and surprising emotions, such as shock, anger, and guilt. Sometimes it may feel like the sadness will never let up. While these feelings can be frightening and overwhelming, they are normal reactions to loss. There has not been one death that I have been connected to that I have not experienced the same feelings. Accepting them as part of the grieving process and allowing yourself to feel what you feel is necessary for healing.

Grief is the emotional state we experience after the death of someone we knew, especially a loved one. Often the most intense grief occurs after the death of a life partner, child, or a sibling and there appears to be a relationship between intensity of grief and the length of the relationship (Cicerelli, 2006). The emotions one might experience vary from numbness and shock. Some people blame themselves which no one should ever do. Many people feel lost and lonely and wonder how they will exist without this other person in their life.

These reactions can appear simultaneously or come in stages. The reactions often persist over the years, although for most these feelings diminish after a year or so for others it may continue for the rest of their life.

No two people from the same family or group will mourn the same person the same way. Even if at the hour of the bad news everyone is under the same roof and learn of the tragedy at the same time the hurt will hit each person differently. Everyone may cry together, but each individual will mourn the loss in their own way. We are all born alone, hurt alone, and will someday die alone.

There is no right or wrong way to grieve but there are healthy ways to cope with the pain. If the grief persist after a year and interferes with a survivor's tasks or daily living, she/he or you might want to seek a counselor who specializes in grief counseling. You can get through it! Grief that is expressed and experienced has a potential for healing that eventually can strengthen and enrich life. I do not want you to read this chapter assuming that I'm attempting to tell you what I have heard; I want you to know that I have had to face my grief as well.

When you enter into grief, you enter into a valley of shadows. There is nothing heroic or noble about grief. It is a painful and lingering process that drains all hope from the human mind. Unfortunately it is necessary for all kinds of loss. It has been labeled everything from intense mental anguish to acute sorrow to deep remorse.

There is a multitude of emotions involved in the grief process that seem out of control and often appear in conflict with one another. With each loss there comes bitterness, emptiness, apathy, love, anger, guilt, sadness, fear, self-pity, and helplessness. These feeling have been described in this way for a number of years.

These feelings usher in the emotional freeze that covers solid ground with ice, making movement in any direction precarious and dangerous. Growth is hidden, progress seems blocked, and one bleakly speculates that just because the crocuses made it through the snow last year is no reason to believe they can do it again this year.

Grief, often become the silent companion for many immediately after death. They experience it psychologically through their feelings, thoughts and attitudes. If it is not handled properly it will impact you socially as you interact with others. You experience it physically as it affects your health and is expressed in bodily symptoms. Your body grieves and mind grieves and grief can settle in for good if there is nothing done to run it out of your life.

Grief encompasses a number of changes. It appears differently at various times, and it flits in and out of your life. It is a natural, normal, predictable, and expected reaction. It is not an abnormal response to a loss. In fact just the opposite is true. The absence of grief is what is considered abnormal. Grief is your own personal experience that no one else can share but you. Your loss does not have to be accepted or validated by others for you to experience and express grief.

Some may ask why grief? Why do we have to experience so awful and what is the purpose for this kind of pain? There are three basic things expressed through grief:

• Through grief you can express your feelings about your loss.

• Through grief you can express your protest at the loss as well as your desire to change what happened and have it not be true.

• Through grief you can express the effects you have experienced through the devastating impact of the loss.

The purpose of grieving over your loss is to get beyond these reactions to face your loss and work on adapting on life without the person that has died. The overall purpose of grief is to bring you to the point of making necessary changes so you can live with the loss in a healthy way. It is a matter of beginning with the question that millions of people ask themselves a year. Why did this happen to me? And eventually getting to a point of moving on to the next question in the grieving stage which is, how can I learn through this experience? How can I now go on with my life? When your how questions replaces the questions, you have actually started to live with the reality of the loss.

Mourning is the necessary process of returning back to life after we have been knocked completely off our feet. It involves leaving behind what need to be left behind, bringing along only what needs to be brought along, and learning to distinguish between the two.

What do you have to do to get to this point? Are there any definite steps you can take so you don't have to guess at the process? Yes there is and I will help you to make those steps. There are four steps that can be followed for most types of losses.

First of all, you need to change your relationship with whatever you've lost. For example, if it was a person, you eventually need to come to the realization that the person is dead and you are no longer married or dating him or her. We have to be able to recognize the change and develop new ways of relating to the deceased person. We can exist without others die. Memories, both positive and negative, will remain with us and there is nothing that can be done to change that. Perhaps we can call this acknowledging and understanding the loss. This can occur with the loss of anything not to exclude a job, home, culture, or a way of life. I will touch more on this in a later chapter.

The next step is to develop your own self and your life to encompass and reflect the changes that occurred because of your loss. This will vary, depending on whether the loss was a job, an opportunity, a relationship, parent, or spouse to death.

The third step is discovery and taking on new ways of existing functioning without whatever it was you lost. This involves a new identity but without totally forgetting about the person, pet or thing that has caused you to grieve.

Finally, you discover new directions for the emotional investments you once had in the lost object, situation, or person. Channel your emotions into new investments. I know that it can be done because I've had to do it myself so I'm here to tell you that yes it does work.

These steps may sound simple but they are not, since all of grief involves work, effort, and pain. Let's consider how these steps can be accomplished. I would say that it is important when we are acknowledging and understanding the loss it's a necessary action to starting the grieving process. Depending on the severity, some losses will soon be a faint memory, whereas others, such as the death of a child or spouse, may never be completely settled. This step does mean integrating the loss into your life.

You must overcome your shock and denial and face the painful reality of what occurred. It means saying, "Yes, unfortunately, this happened." Facing your loss means you don't attempt to postpone the pain, you don't deny that it actually happened. I'm not telling you to minimize your loss, I'm only encouraging you to accept it.

If you do any of these things, you intensify your pain and prolong it which will only make it worse. It may be helpful to admit that you do want to postpone, deny, or minimize your loss. These are normal protective responses. A common myth of grieving is that we should bury our feelings. Expressions such as, "Don't cry," or "Don't feel bad; after all, he's with the Lord now," are damaging myths that does nothing to comfort a grieving person. These things are all too often said by people who feel anxious when a loss occurs because they never learned what to say. I do my best not to use this type of non-supportive statement when I hear that someone has lost a loved one.

To assist in the process, it may help to make a list of the effects of your loss. This is one step in facing your pain. Feel and face all of your emotions. One author suggests that "grieving means allowing yourself to feel your feelings, think your thoughts, lament your loss and protect your pain." [1]

Another step in the process of facing losses is to tell others about it as soon as possible. Don't be afraid to call it by its name: "I just lost the only little brother that I had and I am grieving." You may want to keep track of whom you told, the date, and their response. Some have found it helpful to tell at least one or two people each day during the first week of the loss. It means making the conscious decision that I am going to face it and feel the pain. The best way to describe this kind of pain is intense emotional suffering. You are going home to the uninvited guests of anger, denial, fear, anxiety, rage, depression, and many other uncomfortable emotions but they will not leave unless you demand that they go away.

Sometimes people say they wish they could return to the initial stage of shock or numbness. At least at that point, the pain wasn't so intense. The numbness served as Novocain to remove all the pain. Numbness has been defined as devoid of sensation, devoid of emotion. The exploding bombshell puts many people into a daze.

Depending on severity of your loss, your numb reaction can be a slight down feeling or an incapacitating numbness. Twenty-four to thirty-six hours later it lifts, the pain is faced, and the feelings surge like the seasons of the year. There are seasons of depression, anger, calm, fear, and eventually hope, but they don't follow one another progressively. They overlap and are often jumbled together. Just when you think you are over one, it comes bursting through your door again. You finally smile, but then the tears return. You laugh, but the cloud of depression drifts in once again. This is normal, this is necessary but most importantly this is healing.

The griever's suffering is never constant although at times it may appear that the grieving will last forever. The waves of pain are alternated by lulls of monetary rest. Initially, of course, in acute grief situations the waves are intense and frequent. Gradually, as one is healed are less intense, less prolonged, and less frequent. One can almost imagine the wave patterns chartered on a graph, like radio waves. Each peak represents a mountain of pain, each valley a restful lull. In the beginning, peaks are high and long, the valleys are narrow and short, and the frequency is high. Slowly, the peaks mellow, the valleys lengthen and the frequencies decreases. Gradually, ever so gradually, the storm quiets. Yet months and years later an isolated wave can still come crashing ashore. On sensational holidays, for example, the memories of lost loved ones are often raw.

Tears are the vehicle that God has equipped us with express our deepest feelings words cannot express. I want you to understand that tears are capable of doing and saying what words at times will fail to do.

Before we bid goodbye to those present at the cross, I have one more introduction to make. This introduction is very special.

Grief is a natural response to loss. It's the emotional suffering you feel when something or someone you love is taken away. You may associate grief with the death of a loved one – and this type of loss does often cause the most intense grief. But any loss can cause grief, including:

- A relationship breakup
- Loss of health
- Losing a job
- Loss of financial stability
- A miscarriage
- Death of a pet
- Loss of a cherished dream
- A loved one's serious illness
- Loss of a friendship
- Loss of safety after a

trauma

The more significant the loss, the more intense the grief may be. However, even subtle losses can lead to grief. For example, you might experience grief after moving away from home, graduating from college, changing jobs, selling your family home, or retiring from a career you loved.

CHAPTER 5

Acknowledge You're Grieving

Now that we are familiar with grief, it is important for anyone that is struggling with grief to acknowledge that they are grieving in order for them to understand the mental process that is taking place.

Grieving is a personal and highly individual experience. How you grieve depends on many factors, including your personality and coping style, your life experience, your faith, and the nature of the loss. The grieving process takes time. Healing happens gradually; it can't be forced or hurried – and **there is no "normal" timetable for grieving.** Some people start to feel better in weeks or months. For others, the grieving process is measured in years. Whatever your grief experience, it's important to be patient with yourself and allow the process to naturally unfold.

Myths and Facts about Grief

MYTH: The pain will go away faster if you ignore it.

Fact: Trying to ignore your pain or keep it from surfacing will only make it worse in the long run. For real healing it is necessary to face your grief and actively deal with it.

MYTH: It's important to be "be strong" in the face of loss.

Fact: Feeling sad, frightened, or lonely is a normal reaction to loss. Crying doesn't mean you are weak. You don't need to "protect" your family or friends by putting on a brave front. Showing your true feelings can help them and you.

MYTH: If you don't cry, it means you aren't sorry about the loss.

Fact: Crying is a normal response to sadness, but it's not the only one. Those who don't cry may feel the pain just as deeply as others. They may simply have other ways of showing it.

MYTH: Grief should last about a year.

Fact: There is no right or wrong time frame for grieving. How long it takes can differ from person to person.

Source: *Center for Grief and Healing*

Are there stages of grief?

In 1969, psychiatrist Elisabeth Kübler-Ross introduced what became known as the "five stages of grief." These stages of grief were based on her studies of the feelings of patients facing terminal illness, but many people have generalized them to other types of negative life changes and losses, such as the death of a loved one or a break-up. [2]

The five stages of grief:

- **Denial:** "This can't be happening to me."
- **Anger:** "*Why* is this happening? Who is to blame?"
- **Bargaining:** "Make this not happen, and in return I will ____."
- **Depression:** "I'm too sad to do anything."
- **Acceptance:** "I'm at peace with what happened."

If you are experiencing any of these emotions following a loss, it may help to know that your reaction is natural and that you'll heal in time. However, not everyone who is grieving goes through all of these stages – and that's okay. Contrary to popular belief, **you do not have to go through each stage in order to heal.** In fact, some people resolve their grief without going through *any* of these stages. And if you do go through these stages of grief, you probably won't experience them in a neat, sequential order, so don't worry about what you "should" be feeling or which stage you're supposed to be in.

Kübler-Ross herself never intended for these stages to be a rigid framework that applies to everyone who mourns. In her last book before her death in 2004, she said of the five stages of grief, "They were never meant to help tuck messy emotions into neat packages. They are responses to loss that many people have, but **there is not a typical response to loss, as there is no typical loss.** Our grieving is as individual as our lives."

Grief can be a roller coaster

Instead of a series of stages, we might also think of the grieving process as a roller coaster, full of ups and downs, highs and lows. Like many roller coasters, the ride tends to be rougher in the beginning the lows may be deeper and longer. The difficult periods should become less intense and shorter as time goes by, but it takes time to work through a loss. Even years after a loss, especially at special events such as a family wedding or the birth of a child, we may still experience a strong sense of grief.

Source: *Hospice Foundation of America*

Common symptoms of grief

While loss affects people in different ways, many people experience the following symptoms when they're grieving. Just remember that almost anything that you experience in the early stages of grief is normal – including feeling like you're going crazy, feeling like you're in a bad dream, or questioning your religious beliefs.

- **Shock and disbelief** – Right after a loss, it can be hard to accept what happened. You may feel numb, have trouble believing that the loss really happened, or even deny the truth. If someone you love has died, you may keep expecting them to show up, even though you know they're gone.
- **Sadness** – Profound sadness is probably the most universally experienced symptom of grief. You may have feelings of emptiness, despair, yearning, or deep loneliness. You may also cry a lot or feel emotionally unstable.
- **Guilt** – You may regret or feel guilty about things you did or didn't say or do. You may also feel guilty about certain feelings (e.g. feeling relieved when the person died after a long, difficult illness). After a death, you may even feel guilty for not doing something to prevent the death, even if there was nothing more you could have done.
- **Anger** – Even if the loss was nobody's fault, you may feel angry and resentful. If you lost a loved one, you may be angry at yourself, God, the doctors, or even the person who died for abandoning you. You may feel the need to blame someone for the injustice that was done to you.
- **Fear** – A significant loss can trigger a host of worries and fears. You may feel anxious, helpless, or insecure. You may even have panic attacks. The death of a loved one can trigger fears about your own mortality, of facing life without that person, or the responsibilities you now face alone.

- **Physical symptoms** – We often think of grief as a strictly emotional process, but grief often involves physical problems, including fatigue, nausea, lowered immunity, weight loss or weight gain, aches and pains, and insomnia.

Coping with grief and loss tip 1: Get support

The single most important factor in healing from loss is having the support of other people. Even if you aren't comfortable talking about your feelings under normal circumstances, it's important to express them when you're grieving. Sharing your loss makes the burden of grief easier to carry. Wherever the support comes from, accept it and **do not grieve alone.** Connecting to others will help you heal.

Finding support after a loss

- **Turn to friends and family members** – Now is the time to lean on the people who care about you, even if you take pride in being strong and self-sufficient. Draw loved ones close, rather than avoiding them, and accept the assistance that's offered. Oftentimes, people want to help but don't know how, so tell them what you need – whether it's a shoulder to cry on or help with funeral arrangements.
- **Draw comfort from your faith** – If you follow a religious tradition, embrace the comfort its mourning rituals can provide. Spiritual activities that are meaningful to you – such as praying, meditating, or going to church – can offer solace. If you're questioning your faith in the wake of the loss, talk to a clergy member or others in your religious community.
- **Join a support group** – Grief can feel very lonely, even when you have loved ones around. Sharing your sorrow with others who have experienced similar losses can help.

To find a bereavement support group in your area, contact local hospitals, hospices, funeral homes, and counseling centers.

- **Talk to a therapist or grief counselor** – If your grief feels like too much to bear, call a mental health professional with experience in grief counseling. An experienced therapist can help you work through intense emotions and overcome obstacles to your grieving.

Coping with grief and loss tip 2: Take care of yourself

When you're grieving, it's more important than ever to take care of yourself. The stress of a major loss can quickly deplete your energy and emotional reserves. Looking after your physical and emotional needs will help you get through this difficult time.

- **Face your feelings.** You can try to suppress your grief, but you can't avoid it forever. In order to heal, you have to acknowledge the pain. Trying to avoid feelings of sadness and loss only prolongs the grieving process. Unresolved grief can also lead to complications such as depression, anxiety, substance abuse, and health problems.
- **Express your feelings in a tangible or creative way.** Write about your loss in a journal. If you've lost a loved one, write a letter saying the things you never got to say; make a scrapbook or photo album celebrating the person's life; or get involved in a cause or organization that was important to him or her.
- **Look after your physical health**. The mind and body are connected. When you feel good physically, you'll also feel better emotionally. Combat stress and fatigue by getting enough sleep, eating right, and exercising. Don't use alcohol or drugs to numb the pain of grief or lift your mood artificially.

- **Don't let anyone tell you how to feel, and don't tell yourself how to feel either.** Your grief is your own, and no one else can tell you when it's time to "move on" or "get over it." Let yourself feel whatever you feel without embarrassment or judgment. It's okay to be angry, to yell at the heavens, to cry or not to cry. It's also okay to laugh, to find moments of joy, and to let go when you're ready.
- **Plan ahead for grief "triggers."** Anniversaries, holidays, and milestones can reawaken memories and feelings. Be prepared for an emotional wallop, and know that it's completely normal. If you're sharing a holiday or lifecycle event with other relatives, talk to them ahead of time about their expectations and agree on strategies to honor the person you loved.

When grief doesn't go away

It's normal to feel sad, numb, or angry following a loss. But as time passes, these emotions should become less intense as you accept the loss and start to move forward. If you aren't feeling better over time, or your grief is getting worse, it may be a sign that your grief has developed into a more serious problem, such as complicated grief or major depression.

Complicated grief

The sadness of losing someone you love never goes away completely, but it shouldn't remain center stage. If the pain of the loss is so constant and severe that it keeps you from resuming your life, you may be suffering from a condition known as *complicated grief.* Complicated grief is like being stuck in an intense state of mourning. You may have trouble accepting the death long after it has occurred or be so preoccupied with the person who died that it disrupts your daily routine and undermines your other relationships.

Symptoms of complicated grief include:

- Intense longing and yearning for the deceased
- Intrusive thoughts or images of your loved one
- Denial of the death or sense of disbelief
- Imagining that your loved one is alive
- Searching for the person in familiar places
- Avoiding things that remind you of your loved one
- Extreme anger or bitterness over the loss
- Feeling that life is empty or meaningless

The difference between grief and depression

Distinguishing between grief and clinical depression isn't always easy, since they share many symptoms. However, there are ways to tell the difference. Remember, grief can be a roller coaster. It involves a wide variety of emotions and a mix of good and bad days. Even when you're in the middle of the grieving process, you will have moments of pleasure or happiness. With depression, on the other hand, the feelings of emptiness and despair are constant.

Other symptoms that suggest depression, not just grief:

- Intense, pervasive sense of guilt.
- Thoughts of suicide or a preoccupation with dying.
- Feelings of hopelessness or worthlessness.
- Slow speech and body movements
- Inability to function at work, home, and/or school.
- Seeing or hearing things that aren't there.

Can antidepressants help grief?

As a general rule, normal grief does not warrant the use of antidepressants. While medication may relieve some of the symptoms of grief, it cannot treat the cause, which is the loss itself. Furthermore, by numbing the pain that must be worked through eventually, antidepressants delay the mourning process. If you feel that you need medications to help to cope with your loss please seek the professional opinion of a medical provider.

When to seek professional help for grief

If you recognize any of the above symptoms of complicated grief or clinical depression, talk to a mental health professional right away. Left untreated, complicated grief and depression can lead to significant emotional damage, life-threatening health problems, and even suicide. But treatment can help you get better.

Contact a grief counselor or professional therapist if you:

- Feel like life isn't worth living
- Wish you had died with your loved one
- Blame yourself for the loss or for failing to prevent it
- Feel numb and disconnected from others for more than a few weeks
- Are having difficulty trusting others since your loss
- Are unable to perform your normal daily activities

The stages of mourning are universal and are experienced by people from all walks of life. Mourning occurs in response to an individual's own terminal illness or to the death of a valued being, human or animal. There are five stages of normal grief. They were first proposed by Elsabeth Kubler-Ross in her 1969 book "On Death and Dying." [3]

In our bereavement, we spend different lengths of time working through each step and express each stage more or less intensely. The five stages do not necessarily occur in order. We often move between stages before achieving a more peaceful acceptance of death. Many of us are not afforded the luxury of time required to achieve this final stage of grief. The death of your loved one might inspire you to evaluate your own feelings of mortality. Throughout each stage, a common thread of hope emerges. As long as there is life, there is hope. As long as there is hope, there is life.

Many people do not experience the stages in the order listed below, which is okay. The key to understanding the stages is **not** to feel like you must go through every one of them, in precise order. Instead, it's more helpful to look at them as guides in the grieving process — it helps you understand and put into context where you are.

1. Denial and Isolation

The first reaction to learning of terminal illness or death of a cherished loved one is to deny the reality of the situation. It is a normal reaction to rationalize overwhelming emotions. It is a defense mechanism that buffers the immediate shock. We block out the words and hide from the facts. This is a temporary response that carries us through the first wave of pain.

2. Anger

As the masking effects of denial and isolation begin to wear, reality and its pain re-emerge. We are not ready. The intense emotion is deflected from our vulnerable core, redirected and expressed instead as anger. The anger may be aimed at inanimate objects, complete strangers, friends or family. Anger may be directed at our dying or deceased loved one. Rationally, we know the person is not to be blamed. Emotionally, however, we may resent the person for causing us pain or for leaving us. We feel guilty for being angry, and this makes us even more angry.

Remember, grieving is a personal process that has no time limit, nor one "right" way to do it.

The doctor who diagnosed the illness and was unable to cure the disease might become a convenient target. Health professionals deal with death and dying every day. That does not make them immune to the suffering of their patients or to those who grieve for them.

Do not hesitate to ask your doctor to give you extra time or to explain just once more the details of your loved one's illness. Arrange a special appointment or ask that he telephone you at the end of his day. Ask for clear answers to your questions regarding medical diagnosis and treatment. Understand the options available to you. Take your time.

3. Bargaining

The normal reaction to feelings of helplessness and vulnerability is often a need to regain control–

- If only we had sought medical attention sooner…
- If only we got a second opinion from another doctor…
- If only we had tried to be a better person toward them…

Secretly, we may make a deal with God or our higher power in an attempt to postpone the inevitable. This is a weaker line of defense to protect us from the painful reality.

4. Depression

Two types of depression are associated with mourning. The first one is a reaction to practical implications relating to the loss. Sadness and regret predominate this type of depression. We worry about the costs and burial. We worry that, in our grief, we have spent less time with others that depend on us. This phase may be eased by simple clarification and reassurance. We may need a bit of helpful cooperation and a few kind words. The second type of depression is more subtle and, in a sense, perhaps more private. It is our quiet preparation to separate and to bid our loved one farewell. Sometimes all we really need is a hug.

5. Acceptance

Reaching this stage of mourning is a gift not afforded to everyone. Death may be sudden and unexpected or we may never see beyond our anger or denial. It is not necessarily a mark of bravery to resist the inevitable and to deny ourselves the opportunity to make our peace. This phase is marked by withdrawal and calm. This is not a period of happiness and must be distinguished from depression.

Loved ones that are terminally ill or aging appear to go through a final period of withdrawal. This is by no means a suggestion that they are aware of their own impending death or such, only that physical decline may be sufficient to produce a similar response. Their behavior implies that it is natural to reach a stage at which social interaction is limited. The dignity and grace shown by our dying loved ones may well be their last gift to us.

Coping with loss is ultimately a deeply personal and singular experience — nobody can help you go through it more easily or understand all the emotions that you're going through. But others can be there for you and help comfort you through this process. The best thing you can do is to allow yourself to feel the grief as it comes over you. Resisting it only will prolong the natural process of healing.

The death of a loved one is an event that all of us is likely to experience during our lifetimes, often on numerous occasions. Whilst lives are often transformed by such loss, it does not necessarily need to be for the worse in the long term. Dealing effectively and positively with grief caused by such a loss is central to your recovery process and your ability to continue with and fulfill your own life for the better.

We have put together some notes in this section to help you understand some of the emotions you are likely to go through after the death of a loved one and to offer some suggestions on how best to cope and deal with these emotions.

What is Grief? Am I Grieving?... I'm Grieving.
I can recall as a child my stepfather would use the word grieving very loosely to describe my brother's or my behavior when we dragged around the house. I now know what he considered grieving was our way of expressing boredom from being inside the house instead of being outside playing.

You'll grieve in your own unique way, and a general pattern will emerge as you do so. Those around you may be full of ideas about how you're supposed to grieve, and how not. You may be told that grief comes in clear-cut stages and you may even be given a name for the stage you're supposedly going through. You may hear advice like "Be strong!" or "Cheer up!" or "Get on with your life!" rather than be encouraged to allow your grief to run its natural course. It's important for you to be clear that this is your grief, not theirs. You'll grieve in no one's way but your own.

Grief is about more than your feelings, it will show up in how you think. You may disbelieve this person actually died. You may have episodes of thinking like this even long after they died. Your mind may be confused and your thinking will be muddled. You may find it difficult to concentrate on just about everything. Or you may be able to focus your attention but all you can focus on is the person who died, or how they died, or your life together before they died.

Physical responses are also to be expected. You may experience tightness in your throat, heaviness across your chest, or pain around your heart. Your stomach may be upset, along with other intestinal disturbances. You may have headaches, hot flashes, or cold chills. You may be dizzy at times, or tremble more than usual, or find yourself easily startled. Some people find it hard to get their breath. You may, in addition, undergo changes in your behavior. You may sleep less than you used to and wake up at odd hours. Or you may sleep more than normal. You may have odd dreams or frightening nightmares. You may become unusually restless, moving from one activity to another, sometimes not finishing one thing before moving on to the next. Or you may sit and do nothing for long periods.

Some people engage in what's called "searching behavior"—you look for your loved one's face among a crowd of people, for instance, even though you know they've died. You may become attached to things you associate with your loved one, like wearing an article of their clothing or carrying a keepsake that belonged to them. Or you may wish to avoid all such reminders.

Many grieving people want to spend more time alone. Sometimes they're drawn to the quiet and safety they experience there, and sometimes it's a way of dodging other people. Even venturing out to the grocery store, a shopping mall, or a worship service can feel uncomfortable. There are some people, however, who want to be around others even more than before. You may find that you're jealous of people around you who aren't grieving. You may envy what they have that you don't. You may resent how much they take for granted when you now realize that nothing should ever be taken for granted. You may become critical in ways that are unlike you. Fortunately, this shift is usually temporary.

Some grieving people report unusual happenings that are not easy to describe yet seem very real. You may be going about your daily life and suddenly have a sense of your loved one's presence. Some people report having auditory or visual experiences related to this person. At times the loved one offers a message during a dream or time of meditation. Try not to worry if something like this should happen to you once in a while. Such experiences are more common than you might think. Research also indicates that people's responses during times of personal loss will be influenced by how they're raised, their genetic make-up, and society's expectations. Consequently, some people are naturally more feeling-oriented as they grieve, while others are more oriented toward using their thinking processes. Some respond outwardly, while others keep to themselves. Some want to have a close network of friends around them, and others prefer to be independent.

Ordinary, healthy grief has many possible faces and can express itself in many different ways. You are your own person, with your own personality, your own life experiences, your own relationship with the one who died, and your own understanding of life and death. So you should not expect a "one-size-fits-all grief" that will suit you. You're too unique for that. Despite your individual uniqueness, you'll probably discover an overall pattern to your grief as it progresses. It often begins with a time of shock and numbness, especially if the death was sudden. Everything seems unreal. This is usually followed by a time when pain sets in. Sadness, loneliness, helplessness, and fear may come over you in powerful waves. Anger and guilt may do the same, and continue for a while. In time there comes a slowly growing acceptance of what has happened, but it's not necessarily a happy acceptance.

It's common to feel listless and lifeless, discouraged and sometimes depressed. Other strong emotions can still pop up. This is the winter of your grief—a long, slow, dormant period. In actuality, something is beginning to grow, but its hidden deep underground. A time of gradual reawakening eventually occurs, though you can't always predict when. Energy begins to return. So does hope. Finally there comes a time of renewed life. You're not the same person you were before—you'll be different, having been changed by this experience, having grown. You'll forge a new relationship with the one who died, a relationship that transcends time. This entire process is very fluid. It may not feel very orderly. These time periods will flow into one another almost imperceptibly. But when you look back, you'll recognize what's happened: by going all the way through your grief, you've taken the path toward your healing.

The story of the "bird on the branch"

A tired bird was resting on a branch for support. It enjoyed the view from the branch and the safety it offered from dangerous animals. Just as it had become used to that branch and the support and safety that it offered, a strong wind started blowing and the branch started swaying back and forth, with such great intensity, that it seemed that it was going to break.

The bird was not in the least worried for it knew two important truths. One was that even without the branch it was able to fly and thus remain safe through the power of its own two wings. The second is that there are many other branches upon which it can temporarily rest.

This small example represents the ideal relationship between ourselves and our relationships, possessions and social and professional positions. We have the right to enjoy all these, but cannot as long as we are dependent on them and are afraid of losing them. They are all in a state of change and can disappear at any time.

Our real strength does not lie in those external ephemeral things, but rather on our two internal wings of love and wisdom. These must become our security base, our source of enjoyment and happiness.

Key principles to remember when dealing with the death of a loved one

Accept that loss is a basic part of our life cycle. Whatever is born must die. Whatever grows must decay. These are universal laws. We tend to forget that these physical bodies are mortal. Everything we see around us will one-day decay and cease to be. That includes all plants, animals, people, buildings, cities, the planet earth, the sun and even the galaxy. Everything in the physical universe is temporary. When this fact is understood and accepted, we will begin to seek other, inner sources of security and happiness.

Confront death: We need to ask, "what is death?" What is the nature of that energy, that power, that consciousness which, when it was in that body, caused it to think, speak, move, love, feel and create? Now that it is gone, there is a mass of cells that will soon decompose.

What is life? What is its purpose? A number of us have been forced by the death of the loved one to investigate these questions. Death forces us to look deeper into the nature and purpose of life. Reexamine our life values and goals: Contact with death awakens us to the fact that someday we too will die. This generates a number of questions. Will we have fulfilled our life purpose? Why have we come here to the earth? Why have we taken this physical body? Is our life part of some greater process? If so, what does it require of us? How can we live our lives more in harmony with that purpose?

Answering these questions might motivate us to change our life style, live a more meaningful existence, improve our character, purify our love, or investigate the deeper truths of life. We may also discover that life is more meaningful when we value others and their needs.

How can I help a friend with the death of a loved one
Someone you know may be experiencing grief - perhaps the loss of a loved one, perhaps another type of loss - and you want to help. The fear of making things worse may encourage you to do nothing. Yet you do not wish to appear to be uncaring.

Remember that it is better to try to do something, inadequate as you may feel, than to do nothing at all. Don't attempt to sooth or stifle the emotions of the griever. Tears and anger are an important part of the healing process. Grief is not a sign of weakness. It is the result of a strong relationship and deserves the honor of strong emotion.

When supporting someone in their grief the most important thing is to simply listen. Grief is a very confusing process; expressions of logic are lost on the griever. The question "tell me how you are feeling" followed by a patient and attentive ear will seem like a major blessing to the grief stricken. Be present, show that you care, listen.

Your desire is to assist your friend down the path of healing. They will find their own way down that path, but they need a helping hand, an assurance that they are not entirely alone on their journey. It does not matter that you do not understand the details, your presence is enough.

Risk a visit, it need not be long. The mourner may need time to be alone but will surely appreciate the effort you made to visit. Do some act of kindness it is certain to go a long way. There are always ways to help. Run errands, answer the phone, prepare meals, mow the lawn, care for the children, shop for groceries, meet incoming planes or provide lodging for out of town relatives. The smallest good deed is better than the grandest good intention.

How can I help a child with the death of a loved one?
Children grieve just as adults do. Any child old enough to form a relationship will experience some form of grief when a relationship is severed. Adults may not view a child behavior as grief as it is often demonstrated in behavioral patterns which we misunderstand and do not appear to us to be grief such as "moody," "cranky," or "withdrawn."

When a death occurs children need to be surrounded by feelings of warmth, acceptance and understanding. This may be a tall order to expect of the adults who are experiencing their own grief and upset. Caring adults can guide children through this time when the child is experiencing feelings for which they have no words and thus cannot identify. In a very real way, this time can be a growth experience for the child, teaching about love and relationships.

The first task is to create an atmosphere in which the child's thoughts, fears and wishes are recognized. This means that they should be allowed to participate in any of the arrangements, ceremonies and gatherings which are comfortable for them. First, explain what will be happening and why it is happening at a level the child can understand. A child may not be able to speak at a grandparent's funeral but would benefit greatly from the opportunity to draw a picture to be placed in the casket or displayed at the service. Be aware that children will probably have short attention spans and may need to leave a service or gathering before the adults are ready. Many families provide a non-family attendant to care for the children in this event.

The key is to allow the participation, not to force it. Forced participation can be harmful. Children instinctively have a good sense of how involved they wish to be. They should be listened to carefully. Parents who openly talk about their grief, cry, and express frustration, send a message to their children that it is okay for them to do so. Because children cannot carry the burden of all your pain, try to maintain times for play and talk without conversation about the dead person. Balance, as best you can, the sharing of sad feelings, with the sharing of more pleasant activities and times shared together. This lets your surviving children know how much they are valued.

If your child has had an experience with death, (perhaps a pet, or a grandparent), it may be easier to explain the death to them. Here are some questions which many children wonder about and some suggested answers:

Is death like sleeping? Death is different from sleeping. When you go to sleep your body still works. You still breathe and your heart beats and you dream. When a person is dead, his or her body doesn't work anymore. Remember that children who are told that death is like sleeping may develop fears about falling asleep.

Why did they die? If the death was from an illness, explain that the person's body couldn't fight the sickness any more. It stopped working. Make sure your children know that if they get the flu or a cold, or if mom or dad get sick, their bodies can fight the illness and get better. Their bodies still work. Explain that people do not usually die when they get sick. Most people get better. If the death was from an accident, explain that the person was hurt so badly that his or her body stopping working. Explain that when most people get hurt they can get better and live a long, long time.

Will you die? Will I die? Children are looking for reassurance. Let your child know that most people live for a very long time. Children also need to know who will take care of them if a parent or guardian dies. Let them know who to go to for help if there is a family emergency.

Did I do or think something bad to cause the death? Maybe your child had a fight with the person who died. Maybe your child wished this person wasn't around to get so much attention from other family members. Maybe your child said, "I wish you'd go away from me," or even "I wish you were dead." Reassure your children that saying and wishing things do not cause a death to happen.

Will they come back? "Forever" is a hard concept for young children to understand. They see that people go away and come back. Cartoon characters die and then jump up again. Young children may need to be told several times that the person won't be back ever.

Is she cold? What will he eat? Young children may think the dead body still has feelings and walks and talks under the ground. Some children might imagine a cemetery as a sort of "underground apartment complex." You may need to explain that the body doesn't work anymore. It can't breathe, walk, talk or eat anymore.

Why did God let this happen? Answer questions related to God and your faith according to your own beliefs. You may also want the counsel of your clergy. It's okay to not have answers for everything. Children can accept that you, too, have a hard time understanding some things. It is best to avoid suggesting God "took" someone to be with him, or that "only the good die young". Some children may fear that God will take them away too. They may try to be "bad" so that they won't die, also.

Returning to School
Going back to school following a death can be difficult. You can make this easier by helping your children with possible answers to questions and remarks. Schoolmates may not always be sensitive to your children's feelings. Tell the child that, if they don't want to, they don't have to answer questions. Explain that others may be uncomfortable talking about the person who died. Your home can be a place where you and your child can talk about and remember the loved one. You may want to talk with the school principal, your child's teacher, the school social worker, or counselor, to plan for a surviving child's return to school. You may also want to discuss what information you would like shared with his/her classmates.

Grief work to help effectively deal with grief

Psychotherapists refer to the process a bereaved person will encounter as "grief work." This is because the process is not one that just happens to you, or that will be healed only with time. "Grief work" means tackling some very difficult emotional tasks. Those families who work through these tasks do eventually experience relief from the intense pain. It has been said that there is no way around grief. You must go through it in order to come out of it.

A well-known psychologist, William Worden, Ph.D., has explained the tasks of grief. These tasks are discussed below. Working through your grief can take many, many months or years.

1. Accepting the reality of loss.

When a loved one dies, people often experience a sense that it isn't true. The first task of grieving is to come to the realization that this person is gone, and that reuniting with him or her, at least in this life, will not happen. Some families tell us they sense their loved one's presence through sound, sight, smell or touch. Whether or not these experiences are "real" is a matter of belief. However, they are common and not a sign that one is "going crazy."

2. Working through the pain of grief.
One of the goals of grief counselors is to help people through this difficult time, so that they do not carry their deep pain with them throughout their entire life. Those people who allow themselves to feel and work through the deep pain find that the pain lessens. Some things may prevent this experience. Friends, relatives, and co-workers may give subtle or not so subtle messages to "pick yourself up and go on" as if nothing has happened. Or, sometimes family members cut off their feelings and deny that pain is present. Allow yourself the time to cry or to be angry. Many people find these feelings appear while going through their daily routines such as grocery shopping or driving to work. Know that these experiences, though very hard, are normal.

3. Adjusting to an environment in which your loved one is no longer present
Your loved one had a special place in your heart and in your family. They can never be replaced. But bereaved families can eventually adjust to the absence of a loved one. This process might involve finding new ways of interacting with your surviving family members and friends.

4. Withdrawing emotional energy and reinvesting it in other relationships
Many people misunderstand this task and believe it means forgetting about their loved one. They believe that this would be dishonoring their loved one's memory. This task is simply a continuation of the first three tasks. It involves the process of allowing yourself to make relationships with others. It does not mean that you care any less about your loved one or that you will not keep your special memories.

5. Rebuilding faith, beliefs and values that are tested by the loss of a loved one.
The loss of a loved one can test your faith and philosophical views of life. Talking with a spiritual leader or advisor such as a rabbi, priest, minister or holy person may be helpful since they have experience counseling others who have experienced a loss. Many bereaved families, whom we have known over several years, can remember their loved one and smile. Sometimes there is still sadness, though it does not come as often and is not as draining.

Over time and through these "tasks", you will begin to remember your loved one without experiencing the unbearable pain. It will be a different kind of sadness. Do not hesitate to seek professional help. Counselors are trained to assist you in working through these tasks and other issues you may be facing. It is okay to ask for one session with a therapist to see if you both will be able to work together.

Do's and Don'ts for friends and families when dealing with the bereaved

As a friend or family member, you may not know what to say or how to act. There are few rights or wrongs. There are, however, some things that may be more helpful than others.

Here are a few suggestions that may help you.

1. Just be a good listener. People need to talk a lot about the death of their loved one. The more they talk, the more they process the reality.
2. Don't be judgmental. There is no timetable for completing the grief process. People resent being told "You should be over it by now." Moving toward acceptance is a lengthy process even if people return to work quickly.

3. Talk about the person who died. Don't be afraid to bring up the subject for fear of making the family feel worse. They are already feeling bad and think about their loved one most of the time. They'll know that this person was also important to you and not forgotten.

4. Inquire about the well-being of all family members and loved ones--men as well as women. Men are frequently presumed to be okay when, in fact, they are not.

5. Stay in touch. People will not have the energy to call you. Reach out and make the contact by phone or a personal visit. Invite the bereaved family out for a meal.

6. Don't use clichés. Be honest with your own feelings. If you have trouble thinking of something to say, just be there for the person. You can extend a touch, or send a card. Saying too little is better than too much.

7. Look for an immediate need and fill it. This could be shopping, preparing a meal, answering the phone, baby-sitting, helping with out of town relatives. Check back often to offer support.

8. Try to understand the grieving process. There are many good reference books for sale and in libraries.

Dealing positively with the loss of a loved one

The following list can be very supportive in our effort to cope with the departure of a loved one. If you find any of these helpful, write them down with large letters and place them where you can see them often. Feel free to alter them so that they apply more appropriately to your own specific needs. You could also make a cassette with such messages to play while in deep relaxation or as you fall asleep. Share these thoughts with others.

1. I am an eternal soul and have the power to live an abundant and meaningful life. All is within me. I feel secure, protected and tranquil.

2. My loved one is an eternal, immortal soul who continues to live in another dimension more beautiful than the one in which I currently exist.
3. Since my loved one is very well and far closer to his or her true divine nature, I can be glad for him/her and can give joy to myself and to those around me.
4. Everything happens according to wise and just divine laws which give us the lessons we need for our spiritual evolution. For some reason, it was best for my loved one to move on to another level of existence and for me continue on here, without him or her.
5. Everyone on this earth has lost loved ones. This is a natural and universal aspect of material existence.
6. The departure of the soul from the restrictions of the temporary physical body is a beautiful liberation from a very limited incarnated state.
7. The loss of my loved one is a great opportunity for spiritual development through the cultivation of inner power, tranquility, security and self-acceptance.
8. I accept the perfection of the Divine Laws, and I release God, myself and all others for any responsibility for what is happening to me.
9. My loved one would want me to be happy and to continue my life creatively and beautifully.
10. I am a pure divine being and deserve unconditional love. I am acceptable, lovable and interesting as I am.
11. The loss of a loved one is not related to guilt or punishment but, is instead, a great opportunity for spiritual development and inner growth.
12. No one can be responsible for someone else's death. Each soul has selected the hour and the place when he or she will leave. Others are simply the instruments we use for our departure.
13. I can, even now, correct my relationship with my loved one with inner communication and prayer.

14. I open myself to my brothers and sisters in the family of humanity who are now sharing this planet. My loved one would want me to do so.
15. I share with others my sorrow and joy.
16. I find meaning in myself and my life by relating, serving, creating and evolving.
17. Life is a divine gift and it is my duty to use it to benefit myself and others.
18. Today, 40,000 parents have lost their children. Tomorrow, another 40, 000 parents will lose their children. I am not alone in pain. Departure from the physical body is a natural part of life on earth.

During my time as a Doctoral student at Trinity College, I was given an assignment to do a case vignette on a parent that had loss their child. Below this paragraph you can read it as it unfolded:

There is one universal life force, expressing itself through all beings. The same consciousness that expressed itself through my loved one is now expressing itself through every being around me. When loving and offering to others, I love and offer to him/her as well. Cindy is a fifty-eight year old woman that lost her youngest child to a tragic death that came sudden and with no closure five years ago. Throughout her life, she has lost both of her parents, siblings, nieces, nephews, and a host of other family and friends that were close to her heart and had always been able to move forward and live a normal life, but none of those deaths had the same impact as that of her own child.

She is the mother of three children, whom she has always loved dearly and been very proud of. There was just something about the youngest child Josh that even she couldn't explain. Maybe it was because the fact that he was the baby of the family, or even because she felt a deeper paternal connection to him than the rest of her other children.

After Josh's death, Cindy became extremely depressed and withdrawn from everyone including her remaining two children. She often lashed out and blamed others for the death of Josh whenever she became upset about something, but she is in denial that she is dealing with depression or needs any help. She spent her days and nights confined to her home mostly weeping and sleeping to numb the pain that she was dealing with. No matter what the topic of discussion was about Cindy, would find a way to bring Josh into the conversation which always made her cry and others around her uncomfortable. Those that were closest to her wanted to but just didn't know how to help her to move forward with her life. Her neighbor Mary who was an older woman and someone whom had also lost own her daughter to a very similar death urged Cindy that what she was doing was not healthy and suggested that maybe Cindy should attend a group session for mothers that had lost their children.

Cindy has been coming to group sessions for a couple of weeks but fails to openly talk about her personal experience as a mother who has lost a child. She has been recommended to do individual counseling by her medical physician

Discussion

Prior to her son's death, Cindy had never been a woman that anyone had any reason to suspect of struggling with depression, so although the symptoms are similar to depression they are associated more with grief. There are no outlining symptoms that would conclude that Cindy needs to be placed on medications to deal with her pain.

Using the C-GAS as a basis and following the format of the Pastoral Counseling Treatment Planner. The treatment plan that I feel will better serve Cindy that supports her behavioral description includes long-term, short-term goals.

- Develop a plan to help celebrate the life and the meaning rather than focusing on the death and pain.
- Probe for and reflect any feelings of guilt or blaming of others for the child's death.

- Point out the biblical teachings that sickness, disease, and death are the consequences of the broken, spoiled, and sinned affected world in which we live while God walks with his children through the valley of the shadow of death.
- Articulate feelings of anger, disappointment, and disillusionment about God since the child's death.
- Bring siblings of the deceased to a counseling session to allow them to express their own feelings of grief and anxiety that surround this family crisis. [4]

The outline above is the textbook approach that I used in class, but I want each of you to at least have a general idea on how to acknowledge when others are grieving so they may receive the help that they need.

CHAPTER 6

Finding Peace

It is not always easy to move forward and leave the things or people who mean the most to us behind. For those of us who have lost a love one, we may often feel as if we are the ones who have been left behind. Many people struggle with being able to grow without the person that has passed away primarily because we convince ourselves that we will always have them in our life. It was our plan to watch them grow old until the day that we die. By now we all that thought is just a false hope that can never come true.

Life taught me early and reminds me often that I can't expect for everyone that once was a part of my life always will be there. Yes, it is true that we are all going to die someday but that day does not have to be today and that is why we must learn to find peace after death strikes close to home. In previous chapter, I talked about how death changes life, facing grief, acknowledging death, and other important issues related to surviving death. In this chapter I want to touch briefly on discovering peace in our lives. It simply means to pick up the pieces and do your best to put your life back together once you accept that the other person is not coming back.

We know that death causes an abundance of mixed emotions that at times can be rather unhealthy including unpredictable mood swings. Major depression has been associated with death affects a person's family and personal relationships, work or school life, sleeping and eating habits, and general health.[6] Its impact on functioning and well-being has been compared to that of chronic medical conditions such as diabetes.[7]

A person having a major depressive episode usually exhibits a very low mood, which pervades all aspects of life, and an inability to experience pleasure in activities that were formerly enjoyed. Depressed people may be preoccupied with, or ruminate over, thoughts and feelings of worthlessness, inappropriate guilt or regret, helplessness, hopelessness, and self-hatred.[8] In severe cases, depressed people may have symptoms of psychosis. These symptoms include delusions or, less commonly, hallucinations, usually unpleasant

Maybe you have just wanted to give up and die? Have you ever prayed to ask God to take you out of this old world so you can escape your emotional pain?

I've counseled many others who felt the same way. You are not alone, one of the greatest men in the Bible, a powerful prophet who did many wonderful things for God, got discouraged and was ready to be taken out of this world.

The story goes like this:

Elijah was afraid and ran for his life. When he came to Beersheba in Judah, he left his servant there, while he himself went a day's journey into the desert. He came to a broom tree, sat down under it and prayed he might die. "I have had enough, Lord, " he said, "Take my life; I am no better than my ancestors."

And the Lord came to him: "What are you doing here Elijah?"

He replied, "I have been very zealous for the Lord God Almighty. The Israelites have rejected your covenant, broken down your alter and put your prophet to death with the sword. I am the only one left, and now they are trying to kill me too." (1 Kings 19:3-4, 9b-10).

God answered every other of prayer of Elijah's, but God didn't answer his prayer to die.

Why?

- Elijah had his eyes on the difficulties of his circumstances. He should have kept his eyes on God.
- The prophet let his emotions interpret the seriousness of the situation. Instead, he should have let God intervene and work his will.

In other words, Elijah's eyes and emotions gave him a false understanding of what he faced.

The reality of the situation, according to God, was this: Elijah wasn't alone. Although he didn't know it, God had many words in Israel standing for the Lord. You see Elijah's emotions had so narrowed his focus that he could no longer see beyond himself.

God's power was getting ready to enter the picture and take care of his child. Like many of us, Elijah was looking through the eyes of the hopelessness instead of the eyes of faith.

Can you identify with Elijah? If so, then perhaps God is trying to teach you the same thing that he taught his prophet

- Remember you're not alone; God is with you.
- Keep your eyes on God, not the circumstance surrounding you.
- God's power can change the situation when he thinks it's time.

- Your heavenly Father will take care of you no matter what.

The brain is the control center of the body. The Bible draws an elegant corollary: "The body is a unit, though it is made up of many parts; and though all of its parts are many, they still form only one body. So it is with Christ *(1 Cor. 12:12)*. The brain communicates with the rest of the body in two ways. Through the spinal cord, the brain sends millions of nerve cells into every part of the body.

The body is, in reality an enormous system of checks and balances. If something goes wrong with the system it can give your mind a wrong picture of how you are doing emotionally.

The interplay between the body and the mind is important to grasp as we examine the physical and psychological aspects of depression brought on by death.

It is very important to find peace to avoid listening to the wrong voice or feeling like you can't take the suffering any longer.

"I've had enough, Lord." Have you ever said that? If one of God's greatest prophets, Elijah, voiced those words, you probably have too. Elijah made two mistakes that allowed him to slip into a negative frame of mind:

- Elijah's emotions had become so narrowed that his focus that he could no longer see beyond himself.
- Elijah was looking through the eyes of hopelessness instead of through the eyes of faith.

In the passage Elijah was defeated and unable to find peace because he was depressed after he became the only survivor. He pleaded with the Lord to take kill him. Just like the prophet there are many others that wish that they could also die rather than going through life in pain and without the other person. When you find peace, you find understanding and learn to accept death as a natural function in life.

I know that depression is real and want to share a few helpful tips to combat depression when it seems that it is getting the best of you or someone that you know.

Other ways to help stave off depression include:

- performing some form of physical exercise for at least 30 minutes every other day
- engaging in pleasurable activities or hobbies weekly
- connecting with friends and family
- practicing stress-relieving activities such as deep breathing
- getting between seven to nine hours of sleep each night
- eating a healthy diet
- avoiding alcohol, drugs, and caffeine

God helped his prophet through that dark time, and he wants to help you as well. Widen your focus to see beyond yourself and your hurt. Look at your life and this world through the eyes of faith. Open your heart to the possibility of God's beginning a great work in you and giving you blessing after blessing.

CHAPTER 7

The Power to Survive

Surviving requires the desire to do so, it is not enough to hope that we can make it out of the storm we must also have the will to weather it and survive at all cost. We are taught as small children that we can do anything that we put our minds to and that does not exclude surviving. We simply must make a choice and decide if we are going to stay in the fight, or if we are going to throw in the towel and accept defeat without trying to fight back.

The world did not stop when my father or brother passed away and although things slowed down for me and my family the rest of the world went on with business as usual. Most people are sensitive enough to understand that after a loss that the person that is grieving may need time to cope with the loss so they are typically granted time off to deal with the death. I will tell you that although there may not be a limit of how much time that we need to move forward, life does wait until get ourselves back together fully.

I've had plenty of reasons in life to find a corner to go and lay down in and cry my eyes out, but I have always chosen to stand in the center of the room and deal with each of my issues as they walked into my life. With that thought in mind there is no reason for me or you to surrender our minds or lives after someone is taken away through death. Feeling sorry for myself has never been an option after all what will it do for me? We can either allow ourselves to become overwhelmed and defeated after loses or we can regroup and come out ready to fight.

Out of all the research that I've done and books that I read when I was trying to cope with my experience with death, the book that spelled out what it means to be a survivor came from Norman Wright. In *Recovering from Losses in Life* (Wright, 2006) explained being a survivor as:

1. Survivors plan ahead, if at all possible, so they can be prepared for a transition, loss, or a crisis. Survivors have found a way to cope with and master what they experience.

Life is full of unpredictable transitions that have the potential to become major losses unless the question, how can I best prepare for this and what will it mean to me?

Both men and women go through identity adjustments at fairly predictable stages of life. Those of us that have children will eventually experience the empty nest. For some couples, the empty nest is a major loss and adjustment period. Their sense of a loss and change is very intense and sometimes difficult to deal with. The atmosphere at home changes, and secondary losses are confronted as well. There are fewer choices to make, less confusion and noise. Old patterns of shopping and cooking for additional people will change when there are less people in the home available to eat. My mother still cooks as if all five of her children are still small and ready for a large meal. Truth is new roles have to be established and new pressures may result. Needs that formerly were filled by children will be directed to someone else for fulfillment. Over time my two nephews that my mother raised filled the void left by my siblings and I. These needs include communication, affection, and companionship.

Frequently, the upheaval of children preparing to leave home hits at the same time as the midlife transition or even midlife crisis. There are many studies that show that when the last child leaves home, there is an increase likelihood of martial maladjustments. If this is the case, it's important to anticipate and handle in advance this problem with all of its ramifications. We can either take control of our losses or our losses will somehow take control of us. Learning about grief and it's characteristics in advance as you go through the process of a loss. I want you to take a moment to reflect in what ways have you anticipated changes or losses in your life?

2. Survivors have learned from the wisdom and experience of others. We often do this even before we experience a loss but are also eager to learn during experience itself. We normally don't try to carry the load ourselves but look to others for the insight that we lack.

3. Survivors are not complainers. We handle our feelings well, and even though there may be periodic bouts of feeling sorry for ourselves, we don't whine, grumble, complain, or become bitter. On the surface we seem to have discovered the futility of this attitude earlier in our lives.

4. Survivors have role models. These role models inspire through the way we handle adversity in our lives. Survivors observe what our role models did, and how they did it, and we look very closely at the underlying attitudes. When you see what is possible in others that in itself is what gives us hope.

5. Survivors have a desire to continue to learn and grow. To me it means stretching my mind and attitude to look at something in a new way. It means being willing to branch out and learn something even if you are quite comfortable with what you are doing at that time.

6. Survivors don't blame. Blame is a very easy and common trap to fall into after the loss of a loved one. Often it stems from our feeling of guilt or personal responsibility, even though we were in no way responsible for our loss. If a child dies in a car accident, the parents blame one another, the manufacturer of the car, the doctors, the medics or God. In some losses, other people may be in fact responsible, but fastening our feelings on blaming them will keep us stuck in our grief. Usually blame is uncalled for and has little basis in reality.

7. When a major crisis or loss occurs, survivors are able to develop a way to cope with their loss. They identify the problems and learn to respond as if they are in control. They don't give up on themselves or on life. They come to a place where they are able to say. "Let's see what can be done to survive." I think it is safe to say that all of us feel powerless at times.

8. Survivors find a way to live in spite of what has happened to us. We must find a way to excel in some area or to express ourselves. Since the loss of my brother six years ago, I spend hour's writings to get back the peace of mind that I initially lost when he passed away.

9. Even in the midst of grief, survivors still enjoy life and laugh at times. Yes, it is possible to laugh even when we are hurting. Sometimes we laugh at something a deceased person said or did when alive. My mother and I often laugh at how my brother would tease me when I walked into the house because I'm the shortest male in the family. Gerry, would say "has anyone seen my brother?" as he would look down to the ground or under the dining room table calling my name, as if I was too short for him to see. Often after funerals, there is laughter as people visit with one another to lighten the mood.

10. Survivors have the ability to be flexible and adapt to new situations. They are able to discover strength through adversity and come up with a variety of ways to respond to what has happened.

We don't persist in living just one way but are able to adapt.

11. Survivors have faith in God. Having faith in Jesus Christ and developing a biblical perspective on life is the foundation for survival and recovery. Understanding theology also can help us to accept what happens in life. I don't mean that we always understand it or like it, but we do learn to accept it. Do you understand a cancer ward filled with children under the age of ten? Or the young mothers of a three year old run down by a drunken driver? What about the obedient businessman, who was honest, paid his tithes and his company stilled failed?

Some Christians live by assumptions that are not biblically based. For example:

Life is fair.

I can control what happens to me.

If I follow Christ and His teachings, no tragedy will come to me.

If I am suffering, it is because I am sinning.

If I tithe, God will bless me financially.

It is important to deal with the questions and issues of life and death before the deep hurts of life confronts us unexpectedly. When we don't, too often God gets the blame for us not being ready to except the loss.

Sometimes people need to find a guilty party for their loss, and when they can't find one, they invent one. Sometimes we look at tragedies, shrug our shoulders, and say it is the will of God. We cannot suddenly withdraw from deep reservoirs of faith within ourselves if nothing has been done to nurture our spiritual lives in the past. As human beings made of flesh and blood and bone rather than rubber, steel, or plastic, our reasoning tells us that generally deaths are caused by: errors in human judgment or planning; disease (some of which are self-imposed); genetic disorders; the evil action of others; violence against self; acts of nature such as earthquake, wind, fire, and flood; and unbending natural laws such as the force of gravity.

Our reasoning also tells us that when we violate the God given commandments, which are really positive statements designed to help us live a healthy, uncomplicated life. We create the conditions that can wreak havoc with our personal lives. When we disobey God's laws of health, for example, we can expect sickness and suffering that goes with it. Our bodies are designed by God and require healthful living habits to function properly.

The other side of blaming God is because we have allowed ourselves to believe that we are special because of our relationship with Him or because we have done something for Him, and therefore He will insulate us from the misfortune of life. Truth is we should blame ourselves because God never promised us that the physical body that we were born with was ours for all of eternity.

Pain, death, tragedy, suffering when they hit us we feel tormented and the age old question emerge: Why does God allow suffering? Where is He in our suffering? Does it have any meaning?

We all fear pain, yet from infancy it serves as a warning mechanism within our bodies to protect us from the hot stove or alert us to an inflammatory process within. But when it ravages our bodies, or the body of a loved one, it sears the soul and torments us physically, emotionally, and spiritually. Again we ask *Why does God allow suffering? Does suffering have any meaning?*

When we cry out to God in our times of suffering, we know that we will be heard by one who truly knows what we are going through or have gone through. It is a great comfort for a sufferer to know the presence of an understanding and compassionate God is with them at all times. God does not only invite our very human prayers but also knows what it is like to be in so much pain. God hears, God understands, and God suffers with us.
The source for what we believe has to be the Word of God. When we look at it, we discover that time and time again it states God is good and He has a concern for humankind. We also know that God is omnipotent. That means He is all powerful, but that doesn't necessarily mean everything that happens in the world is the way that He wants it. At the creation of the world, He created humankind with the ability to choose, I would imagine that he left us with this ability so that we would have the freedom to decide how we could make this world better. Due to the choices of people, there are results that are not what God desires. God could not give us freedom to love Him if we didn't have the freedom to reject Him and His teachings.

It is further possible that since God greatly desires individuals who willingly love, worship, and follow Him, He had no alternative but to allow Satan to test them with pain, suffering and misfortune. This is one of the major lessons taught in the book of Job. If you look at the story, Satan had to request permission to test Job from God which God allowed only within very fixed limits (*Job 2:6*).

Recognition of God's self-imposed limitations is the most difficult concept to grasp in this book. Many ardent Christians will have difficulty with this viewpoint. I will tell you that I am convinced that when God created the world, He set laws in motion which even He choose to honor. The problem for us is that these laws interest our lives in the most sensitive areas in suffering and misfortune.

Someone once asked an interesting question in their book "When Bad Things Happen to Good People," Harold Kushner asked:
If God can't make my sickness go away, what good is He? Who needs Him? God does not want you to be sick or crippled. He didn't make you have this problem, and He doesn't want you to go on having it, but He can't make it go away. That is something which is too hard even for God. What good is He, then? [3]
Somehow, joy arises from loss and suffering and toils as much as it does from pleasure and ease. It is much deeper than the surface of existence; it has to do with the whole structure of life. It is the perfume of the rose that is crushed, the flash of color in the bird that is hit, the lump in the throat of man who sees and knows, instinctively, that life is a man's splendored thing.

Don't misunderstand what I have just said I am not suggesting that God sends adversity to enhance our appreciation of life or to make us more aware of His nearness. Nor am I implying that the fullness of life comes only to those who have passed through deep waters. Rather, I am saying that God is present in all of life, including its tragedies. His presence transforms even these agonizing experiences into opportunities for worship.

In one day, Job lost everything including his servants, livestock, his wealth and his children. Job got up and tore his robe and shaved his head. The he fell to the ground in his worship and said: "Naked I came from my mother's womb, and naked I will depart. The Lord gave and the Lord has taken away; may the name of the Lord be praised." Job was smart enough not to blame God with the wrongdoing (*Job 1:20-22*).

We don't worship God because of our losses, but in spite of them. We don't praise Him for the tragedies, but in them. Like Job, we hear God speak to us out of the storm (Job 38:1). Like the disciples at sea in a small boat, caught in a severe storm, we too see Jesus coming to us in the fourth watch of the night. We hear Him say, "Take courage! It is I. Don't be afraid" (*Matthew 14:27*).

If you've lived for any length of time, you've probably had opportunity to see the different ways people respond to adversity. The same tragedy can make one person better and another person bitter. What makes the difference? I would have to say Resources. Inner resources developed across a lifetime through spiritual disciplines. *If you haven't worshipped regularly in the sunshine of your life, you probably won't be able to worship in the darkness.* If you haven't been intimate with God in life's ordinariness, it's not likely that you will know how or where to find Him should life hand you some real hardships. But *by the same token, if you have worshipped often and regularly, then you will undoubtedly worship well in the hour of your greatest need.*

The experience of worship provides the deep resources we need to draw on when everything around falls apart. In worship the emphasis and focus are not on the person but on God. Do you realize that theology will affect how you respond to loss? Your response to life's losses will be directly determined by your understanding of God and how you have worshipped.

We are people who usually put faith in formulas. We feel comfortable with predictability, regularity, and assurance. We want God to be this way also, and so try to create Him in the image of what we want Him to be and what we want Him do.

However, you and I cannot predict what God will do. Paul reminds us of that in (*Romans 11:33*) "O the depth of the riches both of the wisdom and knowledge of God! How unsearchable are his judgments, and his ways past finding out!" (KJV).

God is not uncaring or busy elsewhere. He is neither insensitive nor punitive. He is supreme, sovereign, loving, and sensitive.

I don't fully comprehend God. I too have unanswered question about some of the events of my life. But all of life's trials, and problems, crises and suffering occur by divine permission.

God allows us to suffer. This may be the only solution to the problem that we will ever receive. Nothing can touch the Christian without having first received the permission of God. If I do not accept that statement, then I really do not believe that God is sovereign and if I do not believe in His sovereignty, then I am helpless before all the forces of Heaven and hell.

God allows suffering for His purpose and His reasons. He gives permission for it to enter our lives. This should help us see God as the gracious controller of the universe. God is free to do as He desires, and doesn't have to give us explanations or share His reasons. He doesn't owe us. He has already given us. We look at the problem and losses and say, "Why?" Jesus asks us to look at them and say, "Why not?"

What God allows us to experience is for our growth. God has arranged the seasons of nature to produce growth, and He arranges the experiences of the seasons of our lives for growth also. Some days bring sunshine and some bring storms. He knows the amount of pressure we can handle. In (*1 Corinthians 10:13*) tells us He will "not let you be tempted beyond what you can bear" (NIV). But, He does not always give us what we think we need or want but what will produce growth.

This attitude doesn't negate the pain of loss. When we suffered a loss, we feel like the disciples adrift in that small boat during the storm on the Sea of Galilee. The waves throw us about, and just as we get our legs under us, we're hit from another direction. They struggled on the Sea of Galilee and we struggle on the sea of life. All of us are afraid of capsizing. All we see are waves that seem to grow larger each moment. We're afraid. However, Jesus came to the disciples and He comes to us with the same message encouraging us : " It is I; don't be afraid."

We have all been guilty of questioning God. We ask God, "Where are you?" but he is always there in the midst of the crisis. We ask Him, "When will You answer?" We want Him to act according to our timetable, but the Scripture says, "Be still before the Lord and be patiently for him." The problem is that we become restless in waiting, and to block out the pain of waiting, we are often driven to frantic activity. This does not help, but resting before the Lord does.

You may not feel that God is doing anything to help you recover, because you want recovery now. The instant solution philosophy of our society often distorts our proper perspective of God. We complain about waiting a few weeks or days, but to God a day is as a thousand years and a thousand years an instant. God works in hidden ways, even when we are totally frustrated by His apparent lack of response. We are merely unaware that He is active.

Let us make no mistake about it because God has a reason for everything He does a timetable for when he does it: "For I know the plans I have for you, declares the Lord, plans to prosper you and not to harm you, plans to give you hope and a future" (*Jer. 29:11*). Give yourself permission not to know what, not to know how, and not to know when. Even though you feel adrift on the turbulent ocean, God is holding you and knows the direction of your drift. Giving yourself permission to wait can give you hope.

It is alright for God to ask us to wait for weeks and months and even years. During that time when we do not receive the answer and/or solution we think we need.

CHAPTER 8

Letting Go

In death the funeral is the lasting reminder that a person has left us in life for good and moved on to a better place. It provides an opportunity for the mourners to say their last good-byes. To take a look at the person who is now deceased for the last time while their body is still here on earth, and to express what that person meant to us in the company of our family, and friends.

I often question if we truly ever let the people that we love so dearly in life go after their deaths? How can we let go of the mountains of memories that we have made? It is not the memories that cause us to enter into a state of depression but our selfishness to not allow the deceased to go that hurts us the most. Although I know that letting go is never as easy as it is made to sound, I also understand that it is very necessary to do so.

In a previous chapter I established that everyone deals with death differently and that is expected because we are all very different people. Some people are able to bury their love ones today and go right on living their life without missing a step tomorrow. For others it could be life changing and cause them to never be the same again. Neither way is right or wrong, although I do not feel that death should change the life of the living. I know that no one can tell those affected by death how they should deal with it personally. In the end all we can do is offer suggestions to help others to accept the loss. Only the mourner knows the kind of relationship that they had with the deceased.

It is not my desire to change the way that you feel about the people that has passed on, I simply want to try to offer you healthy alternatives with accepting their death and truly moving on with your own life. You deserve it and they would want you to keep living your life.

My concern is for the millions of people who still hold on to the things of the deceased more than the memories of them. Allow me to explain, many of us say good-bye to the body but never say good-bye to the body of items that the person has left behind. Typically when a parent loses a child you can see this strange behavior. It could be something as minor as leaving the room the way that it was the last time that they child was home to visit. The parent has a tendency to hold on to items that once belonged to that child but many of those things meant nothing of significance to the deceased child. Parents aren't the only ones guilty of this behavior; spouses are often just as bad. How can any of us move on with the future if we spend our time hanging on the past?

The truth is their belongings will never bring them back, and we have to be able to accept that keeping those things will hurt us more than it will help us. Cherish the memories, but let go of the possessions. I will revisit this point later in this chapter and prayerfully then it will make more sense to you.

If you are struggling with letting go of things, I would like for you to try this simple approach:

- take 2 items of the deceased
- hold 1 item in each hand
- get a bag or a trash container
- close your eyes take a deep breath and let them go
- repeat this exercise every week until everything except for your most sentimental items of theirs are gone

Do not be afraid to try this, you are not throwing your memories of them away only the hurt. The more things that we hold on to the harder it is to let go of the person.

It has been a number of years since my father, brother, great grandmother, cousin, aunties and uncles have died and I don't have any items that once belonged to any of them. I don't expect for memories to be enough to satisfy everyone else in the world who has suffered the loss of someone but I can tell you that memories can be used daily and they will never get misplaced like an item will.

I want to share a personal testimony with you on how I know that letting go really works:

I will never forget the day that I received a call telling me that the man who meant the most to me had passed away. I was over my older cousins Lynn and Lemar Jr.'s home sitting on the living room floor when my mother called and told me that my father was found dead in his apartment on the Southside of Chicago by someone who had gone over to check on him. He had been sick for a number of years and even once had a nurse that was assigned to take care of him because his health was so poor. I guess his body had fought for as long as it could fight before it gave up on him and God called him home.

I was Barely 17 years of age but no stranger to death. I had witnessed people die and lost several childhood friends but I had never lost anyone that shared the same bloodline with me. How could the man that was half responsible for my existence be gone so soon?

I did not know him at all in the eyes of many, but I knew him very well because his blood is what flows through my veins. I will be very transparent with you on about my relationship and feeling towards my father. For years I carried a level of bitterness, anger, and what I thought was hatred towards him while he was alive for not being there for me the way that I thought that a father should be.

He and my mother split and went their separate ways when I was less than two years old. He called pretty regularly, so I was familiar with his voice, my mother still had a few photos of him so I was aware of his features. He had a light skin complexion with beautiful green eyes that resembled a cat. I was always told that he was a rather intelligent man who was a gifted artist but never applied himself in the area of art. He had a thing for writing and loved to write long letters.

At the time of his death I had heard all of the good and bad that my father was, but I still felt robbed of knowing anything about him for myself. My two older brothers had gone to stay the summer with him when we were kids so they were able to form their own opinions of him. I could only rely on the stories of others and that created a level of resentment for me against him. As I got older my respect for him declined, I will never forget the day that he called to correct me about my behavior weeks before his death. I expressed to him that he was in no position to tell me what to do because he had never been there for me the way he should have been. I knew that I was not right for the words that I spoke but I was angry and hurt and wanted him to feel my pain. I vowed to him that I would never talk to him again hung up the phone and refused to speak to him whenever he called.

A week or two passed by before I received the news that he had died. Shamefully, I did not know if I was okay for me to be sad, to cry or feel relieved when he passed away. I was not prepared for the death of a parent and not to mention the last conversation that we had was not good. How was I to react to the news of losing someone that I did not know but I knew of as my father? I was confused and although my mind told me not to my heart demanded me to cry because a piece of it was now gone. When he died all of those negative thoughts and emotions went completely away and I was able to do for him in death what I was unwilling to do for him in life by forgiving him.

After nearly twenty years since he was laid to rest, there are still several parts of his funeral that stick out in my mind. I still remember walking into the church and seeing the man that I had so much bitterness towards but yet so much admiration for as his body laid there in the sky blue coffin. It was one of the oddest moments in my life because I felt that I was meeting him for the very first time. As I walked up to view his body, I stopped looked at his face which showed signs of the pain that he once lived with. I touched his hand for the first time in seventeen years and all the anger that I once had for him seemed to instantly disappear. I told my father goodbye and knew that I would never see him again on this earth.

I later discovered that the good-bye that I said to his body at that hour would not be enough to satisfy my heart and provide me with the serenity that I hoped that I would have as I walked away.

Sometimes mourners feel a lingering sadness because others failed to say good-bye in a proper way and I was no different. Some of the events that contribute to incomplete feelings are:

• not enough friends or fellow workers respond with written expression, or they were unwilling to talk about the loss;

• the marker of the plaque at the grave site either was delayed for months or was no appropriate;

- the person conducting the service failed to make the service meaningful because of a lack of information;
- very few people came to pay their respects at the funeral home or the actual service;
- there is no printed memorial service programs listing the person's date of birth and death.

In other situations, similar problems can occur, delaying the completion of one's grief, such as in the following ways

- a lack of recognition for the person retiring or leaving a job;
- a pet that ran away or maybe got stolen, which provided no opportunity to say good-bye;
- others down playing the significance of loss, making it difficult for the person to properly acknowledge it.

I think that it is very important to be able to say good-bye as it provides us with closure and gives us a feeling of still having control over our life and circumstances that was taken away by the loss.

When you say good-bye, you are not acknowledging that you are no longer going to share your life with whatever you lost, regardless if it is a job, home, person, dream, or even a part of your body. You will always have the memory you are simply acknowledging that you will live without whatever it was that you lost.

What helps one person through grief may not be meaningful to others. Some parents who experience miscarriage simply move on with their lives and have no real need for good-byes. Others have memorial services as recognition of the deaths of their children.

Being able to anticipate a loss and how to cope with it still hurts but it is easier to handle because you know that it is coming. It is not uncommon to hear someone exclaim in anger, "I can't believe that he just left me, he never gave me a chance to say good-bye to him."

When my brother Gerry passed away, I called his phone for days just to hear his voice. I was secretly hoping that some kind of way he would answer the phone instead of the calls going to his voicemail. I made the decision that the best thing for me to do was to say goodbye so I could stop torturing myself by expecting for him to answer.

I knew in my heart that I could not continue to go on like that, and I needed to find a way to get closure for his loss. One evening I called his phone and I expressed how much he meant to me, how sadden I was of his loss. I prayed for his soul, told him that I loved him and ended the call by telling him good-bye that was my way of letting go.

.

Maybe you have never considered doing something like this before, but I will tell you that for me it worked better than I would have thought. Again I ask you, whom or what have you said good-bye to in your life? Is there something or someone you need to say good-bye to? No matter when the loss occurred, it is possible even now to still say good-bye.

Although my father has been gone for nearly 20 years and I still wish that I had more time with him. I said goodbye to him a long time ago but I it took a few additional years to let go of the emotions. There are so many questions that I would love to ask him but I came to terms that those questions would have to go unanswered. The day that I laid my father to rest, I found myself with a very odd since of peace. It was not because I was excited that he was gone, it had more to do with the fact that I knew that he was no longer suffering in death the way he had been in life.

My father lived in Chicago for most of his life and all of mine, but when he passed away my grandmother made the decision to have him buried in a small remote town in Mississippi called Coffeyville. From what I can remember the town and the gravesite seemed isolated from the rest of world. I knew even then that his burial location would make it challenging for anyone in the family to go and visit his grave on a regular basis. We drove to what appeared to be miles and miles through the backwoods to get to a rundown graveyard that was filled with graves that had not been attended to for years. The ground was soft and moist, I don't know if it had recently rained or not but I can remember the heavy red mud that we stepped in along the way to his grave.

After the pastor had completed the dismissal, my brother and I stayed behind a few minutes just staring at the baby blue coffin that carried the remains of our father. I knew that there were some things that I needed to get off of my mind and this would be the best chance for me to do so. I told my father what he meant to me, I expressed my own hurt of not having him around the way that I wanted him to be. I told him that I loved him, asked him for forgiveness for the things that I had said to him only weeks before his death. After I said what I needed to say my brothers and I walked away as we left the cemetery.

Over the years I have never gone back to the place that my father was buried. It has been my way of letting go. This may seem odd to some but it works for me. Visiting gravesides does nothing for me, so I do not go. Perhaps this is the very reason that I have no desire to be buried once I die. I've never understood how we return to graveyards that cause us so much grief, but never return to the hospitals that we were born in which was once filled with joy?

Years after his death, I discovered that I inherited something from my father that I never knew of. He was a man of many words and knew just how to make them work for him. Although my father did not really care to talk on the phone for extended periods of time he would write long letters to my siblings and I, to express what he had difficulty with saying. Now that I've been writing for a number of years I can understand why. I would have to guess that his connection to writing had more to do with him having the freedom to pour out all of his truest thoughts and emotions unto paper that his frustrations would not allow him to verbalize properly.

Since I never dealt with certain things with my father properly I found myself in a similar situation with expressing my own feelings towards him. I knew how I felt and what I wanted to say but I just did not know how I would go about saying it. I was frustrated over the fact that he had left me so soon and not to mention, I never had the opportunity to create memories of he, and I.

I decided to write him one final letter sharing some of the significant moments in my life that I wished that he could have been a part of. I even told him about all the things that I wish that he could have been there to stop me from having to go through when I was just a boy. I knew that he would never actually open the letter, but it was still soothing to me to be able to write down all the things that I felt inside. I was letting go of everything inside of me and it felt good.

I now know that one of the best ways to say good-bye to most kinds of losses is in writing. You might be surprised at the different kinds of letters that have been written. The letter is both a way to say good-bye and express the intense emotions that come from a loss.

Over the years, numerous people have written letters to deceased friends, spouses, children, parents, brothers, sisters, and other significant people that they have lost. I think it does the human mind good to come to the reality that those that we loved are now gone. Releasing words on paper is therapeutic and can provide closure in situations associate with a loss.

Besides writing letters, there are other alternatives for saying good-bye. Sending a contribution to a church or charity in the name of the person can be an acknowledgment. Some people set up a living and lasting memorial through a scholarship, by donating a painting, by planting a flower garden or a tree, or by having a plaque made. I will also tell you that just talking to God about what the person who has passed on meant to you is also a great way to heal.

When Christians die, for us it is not a matter of having to say good-bye, but for us it is a matter of being able to say hello to their Lord. This is why our feelings can be a mixture we are saddened for our loss but there is also a sense of joy for what the deceased person is now experiencing. We have a void in our lives, but the deceased person's life is now full and complete. The Christian death is a transition, a tunnel leading from this world into the next.

We need reminders of the meaning of death from the biblical perspective. For the Christian, death is a home going that can only be described as a wonderful journey that ends in beauty. What a joyous moment that will be when we are all reunited with our loved ones who have gone before us. Just imagine if you will, the lines of communication will be reestablished, the old voices heard again, and the deathly silence at the last broken forever – no more goodbyes, no more quick slipping away of loved ones into the mysterious enigma of death.

The most glorious anticipation of the Christian is that, at the time of death, we will come face to face with our Lord and savior. We will not be encountering a stranger, but the best and the most intimate friend that we have ever had. When we think of death as a time of revelation and reunion, we are taught the instantly remove its venom. The Apostle Paul said, *"Oh death, where is thy sting? Oh grave, where is thy victory?"* (*1 Corinthians 15:15*).

I want you to know that letting go is not an easy thing for any of us to do, but just remember that is why God is with us during our moments of need so that He can comfort us during these most difficult times. God will wipe away your tears. He wiped mine and drove my car through five states when I was incapable of doing so. The same hands that formed the world and every piece of nature will caress your face when no one else is around to do so.

The bible declares that every person on earth is appointed to die at some time. Many of us fear it, resist it, try to postpone it, and even deny its existence. I am here to tell you that none of that will work because life on only a temporary stop on our way to eternity. We can all help to bring life into the world but we cannot keep ourselves from dying. Max Lucado's inspirational book *The Applause of Heaven*, concludes his book with home going means with a new perspective:

Before you know it, your appointed arrival time will come; you'll descend the ramp and enter the city. You'll see faces that are waiting for you. You'll hear your name spoken by those that are waiting for you. Maybe, just maybe – in the back, behind the crowds- the one who would rather die than live without you will remove his pierced hands from his heavenly robe and…applaud you for the way that you lived your life.

I won't promise you that letting go will stop you from missing the person that you love, or cause the pain from their loss to just disappear but I can assure you that by letting go you will be able to accept and deal with your loss in a much healthier manner.

Page for Notes

 About the author

Cornelius Jones is passionate in his desire to meet the needs of others. Towards that end he works to help people find the strength they need to move forward in life. Drawing from his own life experiences, Cornelius believes that with the correct tools and teaching anyone can transform their own life.

"Living Life after Death," marks his 7th book since 2010. He is an internationally recognized subject matter expert on relationships, counseling, leadership, social problems and ministry. He is also a speaker and author who continue to soar to new heights in his career as a writer. Cornelius focuses on teaching personal growth strategies to help others through his books.

Also by Cornelius D. Jones

Living Out of Order and Without Favor

Changing the Man Within

Don't Call Me Black, Call Me American

Inspirational Being

Building a Beautiful Relationship

The Power of Marketing You

Appendix

Here, listed are the books I surveyed in preparing *Living Life after Death*. A majority of the content are all of the author's original thoughts and writings after years of research and experience as a grief counselor. Any quoted material is taken from these editions unless otherwise noted in the text.

Holman *Illustrated Bible Dictionary* (Nashville, TN 2003)

Wright *Recovering from Losses in Life* (Grand Rapids, MI 2006)

Sutton & Hennigan *Conquering Depression* (Nashville, TN 2001)

Kok & Jongsma *The Pastoral Counseling* (Danvers, MA 1998)

Savage *Listening & Caring Skills* (Nashville, TN 1996)

Collins *Christian Counseling Third Edition A Comprehensive Guide* (Nashville, TN 2007)

Clinton & Hawkins *The Popular Encyclopedia of Christian Counseling* (Eugene, OR 2011)

Jones *Living Out of Order and Without Favor* (Bloomberg, IN 2010)

Wright *Helping Those in Grief* (Grand Rapids, MI 2011)

Hooyman & Kramer *Living Through Loss*

www.ingramcontent.com/pod-product-compliance
Lightning Source LLC
Chambersburg PA
CBHW030356290526
45785CB00004B/1782